DON BUDGE: A TENNIS MEMOIR

DON BUDGE:

A Tennis Memoir

BY DON BUDGE

THE VIKING PRESS

NEW YORK

First published in 1969 by The Viking Press, Inc.
625 Madison Avenue, New York, N.Y. 10022

Published simultaneously in Canada by
The Macmillan Company of Canada Limited

Library of Congress catalog card number: 69-15661

Printed in U.S.A. by The Colonial Press Inc.

To my mother

I would like to thank Frank Deford
for his help in preparing this book

CONTENTS

1. *"The Greatest Match"* 3

2. *I Learn the First Major Rule for Beginners* 21

3. *Grass and Other Vicissitudes* 38

4. *Learning by Losing* 60

5. *Friends and Foes* 81

6. *The Grand Slam—My Favorite Invention* 101

7. *Turning Pro* 122

8. *Doubles—the Older You Get . . .* 148

Epilogue 168

Appendix 175

Index 182

Illustrations follow page 88.

DON BUDGE: A TENNIS MEMOIR

1

"The Greatest Match"

However hesitant I am to try to select the various "greatest" moments in my career—the best this, the most thrilling that, and so on—I certainly have no difficulty in naming the greatest match in which I ever played. It seemed to possess every element that could be called classic. The players, winner and loser alike, were only part of the whole scene. It was, simply, a supreme day for tennis and a triumph for all that the sport can mean.

There was high drama in every way. It was, first of all, crucial, a deciding Davis Cup match. It was competitive, long, and close. It was fought hard but cleanly by two close friends. It was cast with the ultimate in rivals, the number-one-ranked amateur player in the world against the number two. It was placed in the perfect setting, at Wimbledon, on the Centre Court, a piece of land that is revered in the game. There was a filled stadium. Queen Mary was on hand. Hitler listened intently to the play-by-play, and so did so many Americans that stock-market sales sagged during the action. There was so much that I think that day would have been well-remembered even if the tennis had been pedestrian. There are other tennis legends that I have been involved in that are no more than that— legend, not truth—but I honestly do not think that anyone has ever had to embellish upon what actually happened when Baron Gottfried von Cramm of Germany and I played in the Interzone Finals of the Davis Cup on July 30, 1937.

As one of the participants, I have, of course, always found it impossible to evaluate objectively all that happened on the court that day and place everything in the right perspective. I do know, though, that I never played better and that I never played anyone as good as Cramm. Walter Pate, the United States team captain, said later, "No man, living or dead, could have beaten either man that day."

I realize too that a great many sports events get better and eventually find greatness with time and the retelling, but there was instant recognition of the quality of this match. It was, in fact, Bill Tilden himself who I first heard declare that it was "the greatest tennis match ever played." He told me that, emotionally, clasping my hands, in the locker room only a few minutes after it was completed. The London *Times* correspondent wrote the next morning, "Certainly I have never seen a match that came nearer the heroic in its courage, as in its strokes, as this."

I suppose it was an hour or so after the match before I was at last able to dress and leave the locker room. I think it was almost nine o'clock by this time, but the midsummer sun wasn't down yet. I walked out and glanced up into the stands, and I was shocked because there were still thousands of people there, clustered together all over the stadium. It did not seem to me that they were talking much to each other or moving around. They did not seem to be ready to leave. It was as if they just wanted to stay there where they had watched the match. I've never seen anything like that, before or since, just all those people standing there and remembering, long after I had dressed and gone.

For weeks after the match I would often wake up in a sweat, dreaming of it again. In some way, it seemed to touch all of us who were part of it. So I know that the years have not honored the match as something better than it was. Obviously it is not for me to say whether it was truly the greatest match ever played, but I am sure of this, that however history will rank it, it was something very special.

It was already late in the afternoon, nearing four o'clock, when Gottfried and I at last moved out onto the court, to bow to Queen Mary and to play. Henner Henkel had just beaten Bitsy Grant in four sets to tie the score at 2-2 in the match between the United

States and Germany. Gottfried and I, the two ranking amateurs in the world, were to play for it all.

The winner of the Interzone Final still would have to meet England, the defender, in the Challenge Round, but in just about everyone's view the winner of the 1937 Davis Cup would certainly be the survivor of the United States–Germany meeting. Fred Perry, who had led the English to victory in the competition for the previous four years, had turned pro, weakening the British team to a point where it would be a definite underdog against either of the challengers.

Thus it was, that if I won this one match the United States would almost certainly get the Cup back across the Atlantic after a full decade in Europe. On the other hand, if Cramm beat me, the Germans looked just about as certain to win their first Davis Cup ever, a point not lost on Hitler himself, as it turned out. Perhaps he was still fretting about Jesse Owens.

Cramm was of the old German nobility. Whereas I had grown up learning tennis on the courts at Bushrod Park in Oakland, California, Gottfried had learned with such people as King Gustav of Sweden. But his real nobility was in his human qualities, rather than his lineage; he was one of the finest sportsmen in the world and perhaps the most popular of all the players. He also loved tennis. This match was to be one of his more than a hundred Davis Cup matches. As late as 1953 he was leading the West German team, and his strokes, like his honor, were so beautiful that he was always a threat, wherever he played.

As it turned out to be a match of such significance, it was only right that it should be staged at Wimbledon. I do not believe that any other sport possesses anything comparable to Wimbledon. It is a shrine and dripping with tradition, but the memories never dull the present. On the contrary, at Wimbledon the tradition seems to breathe life into the everyday and make it more significant. Besides, the courts are of the highest quality and the fans are the fairest and the most knowledgeable, so that it offers the finest in neutral surroundings, which was important this afternoon when a German and an American were playing.

I think that I realized early in the match that the crowd was slightly in favor of Cramm, but I could not be either surprised or disturbed at that reaction. The British fans had always been more than fair with me. Now, though, I was the only logical villain, for everyone loves the underdog and Gottfried was that even if he was number two in the world. I had beaten him in straight sets on this same Centre Court in the finals of the Wimbledon tournament only a couple of weeks earlier. Besides, and more to the point, the British team was supposed to have a slightly better chance against Germany than against the United States. Rooting for Cramm was sensible as well as sentimental. Maybe this was the last afternoon for a long time in which they cheered for a German in London. I never played Gottfried at Wimbledon again. Long before the next July the Nazis had trumped up some charges against him, rushed him through a kangaroo court, and put him in jail.

Of course I did have many English cheering for me, and I knew that I had a spirited American coterie rooting me on. Paul Lukas, the movie actor, had just about become an unofficial member of our team in the weeks before, and he had brought Jack Benny and Ed Sullivan along to the matches. I also had at least one American against me: Bill Tilden, who was the professional coach of the German team. Still, as the match wore on, I got the feeling that there was no one present who was really *against* either of us. It seemed that the longer we played, the more exciting and better the tennis became, the less the crowd really cared who won. The art of the match, and the competition, seemed to become much more important than the outcome. Here we were, the best two amateurs in the game, playing for both the individual and the national championships of the world, and playing on the most important court in the world, and yet somehow the magnificence of the game of tennis prevailed over all.

The ironic thing about the match was that right up to the time it started I had had hopes that it really wouldn't have to count for a thing. The matches with Germany had begun three days before, a Saturday. On this opening day Cramm whipped Grant in straight sets and I managed the same against Henkel. Then, after Sunday off, Gene Mako and I teamed up in the doubles Monday to beat Cramm and Henkel in four sets. We were very fortunate, for they had good leads in each of the three sets we won. But we won, so when I came into the locker room Tuesday before my match, I was hoping that Bitsy could beat Henkel, put us ahead 3-1, and make my match against Cramm relaxed and *pro forma*.

Unfortunately, however, Henkel defeated Bitsy easily, and before I really had time to console him, Teddy Tinling, the tennis-clothes designer, who was acting as sort of a sergeant-at-arms, was there in the American locker room, calling me. The main part of Teddy's job this day was to move things along at a brisk pace. The Royal Box was filled with Royal Family, and it was not to be kept waiting. In hardly any time at all, Tinling had me by one arm and Cramm by the other and was marching us off to play. Gottfried and I were bustled along so that we hardly had time to acknowledge each other, and Tinling had just about swept us out into the stadium when a phone rang. None of us paid any attention, but a locker-room man picked it up and called to Gottfried. "Mr. Von Cramm," he said. "Long distance for you, sir."

"Come on, you can't keep Queen Mary waiting," Tinling said, tugging at Cramm, and myself, as well.

"But it might be an emergency," Cramm replied. I had to sympathize with Gottfried. As much as I would hate to get a long-distance call just before a match, I think it would be even worse to get a call but not take it and spend the whole match wondering who it was and what in the world it was all about. Tinling frowned but let Cramm pull free and go over and pick up the receiver. "Yes, hello," he said. "This is Gottfried Cramm." He spoke impeccable English, just as he did a half-dozen other languages. Teddy and I relaxed and did not pay much more attention until Gottfried finished speaking to the operator and suddenly switched to German. "Ja, mein Führer," was the first thing he said.

He said, in fact, little else but "Ja, mein Führer" for the rest of the conversation. He was firm throughout, though he spoke with respect. He showed no emotion. Teddy and I (and Hitler, for that matter) knew that Gottfried was less than enchanted with the

Nazis. Finally, after a couple of minutes or so, Cramm hung up, turned sharply and walked over to Tinling. Teddy handed him his rackets back. "Excuse me, gentlemen," Gottfried said matter-of-factly. "It was Hitler. He wanted to wish me luck." That was all he offered, and there was time for no more. In a few steps we were marching into Centre Court, with the crowd rising and roaring all about us.

At this time, only a couple of weeks after I had beaten him to win my first Wimbledon, it was I who was clearly the favorite. Yet no matter how proud and confident you might feel—and I was, believe me—whenever you walked onto a court with Cramm, it was difficult not to feel that you were walking in his shadow.

I think the reason he irritated the Nazis so particularly was not so much just that he refused to go along with them, but that he looked and acted like the Nazis' propaganda said all Germans should. He was six feet tall, with blond hair, of course, cold blue eyes, and a face that was handsome to a fault. And more, Gottfried emitted a personal magnetism that dominated any scene he was a part of.

Later that year, in September of 1937, he came to Los Angeles to play in the Pacific Southwest Tournament. Most of the box-seat holders—I believe it was as much as eighty per cent of them—got together in advance and agreed that in order to protest against the Nazi government, they would stand up and walk out of the stadium as soon as Cramm entered the court for the first time. Most of the movie people involved were enthusiastically behind the idea. So Cramm came out for his first match. They all looked at him, and even though they were all pledged to stand up and leave *en masse*, not one could make the first move.

They just looked at him and then at each other, and they suddenly found they could not do it to him. "When I saw that man, I just felt instant shame at what I was supposed to do," Groucho Marx told me later. And, of course, they were all relieved that they had not carried out the insult when they found out the next year that the Nazis had imprisoned Cramm. The Nazis eventually let him out, put him in the army, and sent him to the Russian front. At the time, the Germans desperately needed men of his training to be officers, but they sent Cramm to Russia as an enlisted man. He promptly won the Iron Cross for bravery. After the war Gottfried won another kind of fame for marrying Barbara Hutton. He also became a very successful cotton broker in West Germany. In 1947 he was cleared by a special court of all the weird charges brought against him by the Nazis.

We still occasionally see each other. I can remember when I first met him, at Wimbledon in 1935 when I was nineteen years old and the ninth-ranked American, and suddenly found myself in the semis against Cramm, who was already second in the world to Perry. He sought me out on the players' porch and introduced himself as my next opponent. "Don," he said, as if I had no idea at all, "I'm Gottfried Cramm." He not only never used the "Baron," he never even used the "Von." The first thing we talked about was sportsmanship, which was appropriate, because he was, simply, the greatest sportsman I ever encountered. There was no one even close to him.

In 1935, for example, in the Davis Cup Interzone matches against the United States, Cramm and Kay Lund had Wilmer Allison and John Van Ryn at match point in the doubles. The Germans appeared to win the point and the match until Cramm volunteered that the ball had illegally nicked his racket. It cost Germany the match. But he was that way. From that first day I met him on the porch at Wimbledon he became one of the greatest influences upon my life. Gottfried Cramm's ideals bordered on being beautiful. I mean that.

This day in 1937 it was obvious to me as soon as the match began that his game this day was at a level with his demeanor. It was as if he was determined to make up for all his previous disappointments on this court, where, for three straight years he had lost in the Wimbledon Finals—twice to Perry, this year to me. I realized very quickly that I would have to improve substantially on that last performance of mine were I to beat him again. Fortunately, I had no idea then how much I would have to improve.

Cramm had won the toss and elected to serve first, which as it worked out, was to be the case in each set. He held that first serve at love, I came back to win mine at thirty, and we moved on that way, sharing service through the first eight games. In the ninth, I broke through. I didn't know it then, of course, but this was to be the longest game in the match—until the very last one. But then, at that time, ahead 5-4, I just felt pretty good. Hold my serve, take the set 6-4, and I'm winging.

There was no reason, either, why I shouldn't hold serve. It was moving well, I was getting it in deep, and Cramm had not been able to take more than two points off it in any game so far. Besides, I had fresh new balls. And the fact is that my reasoning was absolutely correct. I *did* serve well in the whole game. I held up the new balls and showed them to Cramm across the net. Right away, I smashed a beauty at him. It clicked right in. I never touched his return. I moved over and hit another beautiful first serve. I never touched his return. I hit another beautiful first serve. I never touched his return. I hit my fourth straight beautiful first serve. As a matter of fact, the only thing I hit in the game was beautiful first serves. And that was all he hit back. I never touched the fourth return either. Cramm had broken me back at love with four fantastic placements. I did not win the set at 6-4. He broke me again four games later, and *he* won the set 8-6.

The second set was much like the first, only now, increasingly, it was his serve that was dominant. I was holding my own and matching him, but with more difficulty. Tactically, we were both playing well, but he was having more success at getting to the net and staying there. He attacked incessantly, and kept me on the run and tried to exploit a bad patch of my forehand that showed up here.

For my part, as the set wore on, I found it more difficult to get to the net at all behind my serve. Eventually, I had to give up trying to do that altogether. Cramm was, as always, in such excellent condition that it was foolish of any opponent of his to introduce any waste motion into the game. By trying to rush the net after I served I was using many extra steps and a lot of extra energy every time I faulted and had to go back again for my second serve. And besides, the serves I hit that did go in—well, he was passing me with a lot of those anyway.

Therefore, I decided to put all the extra effort into the serve, hit it really hard, and lie back and try to take his return on the rise. Then I would attempt to come in to the net. This worked well, but I still had no defense for the placements he kept drilling past me no matter where I was. It was becoming a little discouraging. I was sure that I was playing tennis as well as I ever had before, but here I was one set down and struggling to stay even in the second. The fewer mistakes I made, the fewer still he made, and he held serve to 6-5.

Then in the twelfth game I roared right out to forty-love, but I let him off the hook and he took the next three points to catch me. We battled through two more advantages, and then for the first time, Gottfried got the advantage—and set point. He played to win it. He followed my serve in to the net and then took my return with a go-for-broke volley that swept past me and chipped the chalk off the back line. I was down two sets to none.

At this point I remember becoming more mad than analytical. Two things, in particular, kept going through my head. The first was that I was rapidly blowing what had been a very good chance to establish myself as the acknowledged number one in the world, the champion. Secondly, I knew I was doing what so many other Americans had done in past years: come over to Europe, fare well at Wimbledon, and then play poorly in the Davis Cup. That was the one thing I had promised myself not to do, but I certainly was doing it. I called myself a lot of names.

At any rate, whatever I was thinking must have been right for me, for I promptly went out and broke his serve in the first game of the third set. For the second time in the match I was ahead, and I held on to 2-1. At this point I was serving, I had new balls, and I immediately fired off a beautiful batch of first serves. If all of this sounds slightly reminiscent of something else, it was. Exactly as in the first set, the last time I had been ahead, he blasted back four straight passing shots, broke me at love, and tied up the set. I was the unwitting pioneer of the instant replay, and to say it shook me up would be every bit of the truth. Happily, it was all so astounding, I think that it also shook up Cramm. I came right back in the next game and broke *him* at love. Touché. I finished out the set at 6-4, and hurried off to the locker room for a welcome rest.

It was a warm, humid day, with just a touch of wind, the way warm days in England always are, and I was glad for the chance to take a quick shower and change into fresh clothes. Beyond that, there was little I could do. I don't remember talking to Captain Pate about much at all. How, after all, could I improve? Most matches, you know, are considered to be excellent technical performances if the number of winning placements equal the number of errors. In this match, both Gottfried and myself were to make *twice* as many placements as errors.

As a matter of fact, the only time in the whole match that one of us played poorly was when Cramm slacked off right after this rest period. I not only broke him at love in the first game, but I held my own serve and then broke him again to go ahead 3-0. Behind that much, Cramm then decided to junk the set and to try to save all he had for the final one. We went through the motions of playing it out to 6-2, and then he picked up the balls and began to serve in the fifth set, fifth match. The sun was still up and we would finish that night.

It was the first time I had ever played Cramm in a fifth set. I had a pretty good record in five-set matches, but his was unbelievable. He trained so hard and maintained such superb shape at all times that he often said that he figured that he had about a three-to-one advantage anytime a match entered a fifth set. If I had to be reminded of this fact, I knew that only a few days before he had won the key match against Czechoslovakia in the finals of the European Zone by the score of 3-6, 4-6, 6-4, 6-3, 6-2. Perhaps even more impressive than that, Cramm had won the French championships the previous year by lasting to five sets in almost all of his matches, and then finishing it off by beating Fred Perry 6-0 in the fifth set of the finals. This particular victory had, by itself, resulted in giving Cramm an almost mystical edge in long matches. Of course, he was a man of such tremendous bearing and presence that the other players seemed almost eager to present him with capabilities that possibly he did not truly possess. If you were the opponent, however, coming into a fifth set it was not easy to ignore the mystique.

In this instance, while I could not be overcome by Cramm's fifth-set reputation, neither could I be deluded by his poor performance in the fourth set. I imagined that he was playing possum. Certainly, I never considered that he was tired. Perhaps Gottfried did become tired or hurt like the rest of us, but if he did he never showed it. The year before, in the finals at Wimbledon, I had seen Perry beat Gottfried 6-1, 6-1, 6-0. Obviously, something was terribly wrong with Cramm, but he never let on.

Afterwards, he admitted to the locker-room masseur that he had pulled a hamstring muscle in the second game of the first set. Instead of defaulting or asking for aid or seeking some solace in excuses, all he would do was apologize to Perry and the spectators for his poor performance. I pulled a hamstring once playing baseball, and it was all I could do to get out of a chair. Cramm didn't even seem to limp.

So now, as we entered our fifth set, I knew quite well that he would give no indication if he was tired. It didn't take me long to find out that that wasn't even worth speculating about. He took charge from the first, picked up momentum, broke my serve in the fourth game, and held his to move ahead 4-1. He had only to hold serve to run out the set easily.

In the stands there was a new, excited buzz, one of obvious anticipation. I did not notice it myself at the time, but in one section of the stadium, over where the other players were seated, there was an even livelier response. I was to hear about it in the greatest detail later.

It revolved about Tilden, who was the German coach. He had long been something of a private tutor to Cramm, and was close enough to him so that he often stayed in the Cramm family apartment when he was visiting Berlin. It was Tilden who had taught Gottfried to adjust his backhand grip in 1933, and the change had played a significant role in Cramm's rise to top world-class rank. Now Tilden was coach of the whole German team. It is, of course, not at all unusual for a pro in one country to coach another nation's Davis Cup team. But it is uncommon for a coach to maintain the post when it means working against his *own* nation. That is extraordinary, and a lot of people considered it, if not downright unpatriotic, at the least a little tactless of Bill.

But if his loyalties were divided, Tilden made it plain enough that his tennis allegiance was strictly with his employer. He was seated a few rows in front of our team's show-business friends—Benny, Sullivan, and Lukas. They in turn were a few rows in front of Henner Henkel, who had come back to watch our match after beating Grant. Now, with Cramm ahead 4-1 in this last set, Tilden could not contain himself any longer.

He stood up in his seat and turned full around, looking up past Benny and Sullivan and Lukas to where Henkel was sitting. Tilden drew Henkel's attention, and then, without a word, but with only a large smug grin on his face, Tilden held up his hand, forming a circle with his thumb and forefinger—the traditional "it's in the bag" sign. Sullivan and the others saw it right away and were furious. Immediately, Sullivan leapt to his feet and began to try to tear his coat off. "Why, you dirty sonuvabitch," he hissed at Tilden. Lukas and Benny jumped up themselves and managed to pull Sullivan down and hold him. Tilden just smiled back and then sat down again, contented.

At this moment, out on the court, I was changing sides with Gottfried. I kept thinking: Is he really this invincible in the fifth set, am I going to go down just like all the others? Walter Pate threw me a towel, and I rubbed myself with it. "Don't count us out yet, Cap," I told him, perhaps with more courage than logic. "Look, I'm not tired and I feel great." And that was the truth. I won my serve at love and came back to 4-2.

I was at the net when I took the last point in the game, and in the walk back to receive serve I decided that it was time for me to try something new. The thought just struck me quickly that way; I really had no idea *what* I should try. But, after all, I could no longer take any solace in the hope that playing better than Cramm would reward me with the win. We were both playing too well, and I was the one who was two games from extinction. I had to get lucky and I had to make my own luck. Okay, without thinking too much about the odds, I planned to play it half-safe and gamble on his second serve. I decided that if he missed the first one I would creep up several steps and attack his second serve, and then come to the net quickly behind it.

Looking back, I can't really consider this good strategy, because Cramm had such a controlled first serve that it was seldom that he did not get it in. Even when he missed, it was invariably off by only a hair. But if he missed—ah, *if*—well then I was in good shape because his second serve was pretty well typed for me. His second serve tended to be a high kicker. Against most players it was terribly effective, but in my case it just so happened that I had the type of backhand that made it possible for me to pick up the serve on the rise before the ball could take off on that big bounce. Also, moving up a couple of steps in advance of my usual position gave me that much better opportunity to hit the ball before it took the big hop. This also put me in better shape to rush the net afterwards. When I had been playing my normal, deeper receiving position, I couldn't force him enough to permit me to come rushing up and try to gain the net.

I have often wondered what happened to Gottfried at this point. Maybe I just got lucky with the law of averages. But I remember how anxious he was to get the balls to serve, and I think perhaps that he became just a little too impatient. The victory was so close now that perhaps for once in his life he lost the composure that he always guarded so well. But anyway, his first service, which had been so consistent throughout the match, failed him every time but one in this game, and that one serve was to be the only point he won. The other four times he served, he missed getting the ball in by just about the same slim margin each time. Each hit in almost the identical spot, at no more than two inches back.

And each time, of course, that gave me the chance to employ my new strategy. I moved up for that second serve. And located there, as I figured, I was able to catch his second serve before it could bounce up and away. I hit each one back, hard and deep, putting Cramm on the defensive and myself at the net. Each of the four points that I won were made exactly the same way with a well-placed net volley on my second shot. I had the break I had to have, and I was back to 3-4.

He almost came right back and broke me in the next game, but twice in a row, as the score stood at his advantage, he punched backhands that went out, in the same spot, by inches. How many times in this match did these crazy things repeat themselves? After this sort of double jeopardy, I managed to hold and to tie the score at 4-4. As the tension grew to almost unbearable proportions, we matched each other's serve to 6-all. Then, remarkably and suddenly, and without, really, any shots of distinction, I broke Cramm in the lucky thirteenth game and stood ahead for the first time in hours, 7-6.

Now, at last, I had only to hold my serve to win the match and the opportunity for the United States to play England in the Challenge Round. Clearly, after hours of play, I was now immune to pressure. This is why my first serve in the game went right smack into the *bottom* of the net. That either steadied me or embarrassed me, for I did manage to get the second serve in and even to win the point. He tied at 15-all, and then we repeated the sequence: 30-15, 30-all, and 40-30, the first match point of the long afternoon.

So, I guess, I played it too safe again. I was too tentative with both my serve and second shot. Cramm took the net easily, volleyed past me, and we were deuce. I came right back with a placement of my own for a second match point, but he took the net away from me again and once more tied the game. Moreover, when he was able to repeat the ploy on the next point, he moved ahead. Later, he also had one more game point, so that by the time I gained my fifth match point it was the eighteenth point of the game, and all of five minutes had passed since we had first played a match point way back there at 40-30. Five minutes under circumstances like these are like a month of 3-2 counts in baseball.

So once more I served. It was the 175th time that day I had made a first serve. What there had been of my cannonball had gone, but I managed to get enough on this one to clear the net and send it sufficiently deep so that Gottfried could not begin to move up and gain the net from me. But he made a beautiful long return that kept me far back in the court too. All I could do was trade long ground strokes with him. I hit a good backhand.

Cramm moved over to his right-hand corner, so that we were now both on the same side of the court, facing each other down my left-hand side. He caught my shot with a forehand and hit it cross-court. It was a beautiful shot, firmly hit, and it gave him the opening to move toward the net. He came up, crossing the court catty-cornered, following essentially the direction of his shot.

The ball was landing just inside my right sideline, a bit deep of mid-court. I had hit my last shot far back on the other side of the court, and I had begun to move back toward the center as soon as I hit it. Now, however, when I saw Cramm place the ball so far over, I had to break into a dead run if I wanted to catch up to it. I could not worry about position at all any longer. In fact, as I neared the ball, just as it bounced in, I realized that my speed had brought my body too far forward. There was no way I could brace to hit the ball. As a matter of fact, there was suddenly no way I could keep from falling.

Instead, resigned to this indignity, I did the only thing I could. I kept going at full speed and just took a swipe at the ball. What did I have to lose? I was going to fall anyway. Then, immediately after I swung, I dived for the ground, preparing to break my fall. I could tell, though, as soon as I hit the ball that I had smacked it solidly, but only as I crashed onto the grass did I turn to look. The ball whipped down the line, just past Cramm's outstretched racket. He had come up fast and could cover all but about the last two feet on the right side of the net (his left). At my angle I could not have returned the shot cross-court. I had been forced to try for a shot right down the line. Now I saw the ball slip past his reach.

By this point I was flat out on the ground, but so far outside the alley line that I could see around the net into much of the other side of the court. I could see the ball hit. I watched it kick up. But I had no perspective and no idea where the ball had landed. I waited for the call and then, suddenly, even before the linesman could begin to flatten out his hands in the "safe" sign, I could hear the cheers begin to swell. They were different cheers. The ball had landed, miraculously but perfectly, in the corner. I had hit the one possible winning shot. I was told later that the ball landed at a point less than six inches from being out *two* ways—to the side and long.

But now the roars were greater and more excited, and here I was, still lying flat out on the ground. Gottfried, the noble loser, had to stand at the net, waiting patiently for me, the winner, to get up off the ground. I rose, finally, bewildered, and rushed toward him. I tried to hug him, but before I could he stopped me and took my hand. "Don," he said, evenly and with remarkable composure, "this was absolutely the finest match I have ever played in my life. I'm very happy that I could have played it against you, whom I like so much." And then he pumped my hand. "Congratulations." Only then was it, at once, that we threw our arms about each other. I think we both wanted to cry.

I know I was still in a daze in the locker room. It was as if everyone was trying to outdo each other in congratulating me. Tilden came in, and it was right then that he came over and told me it was the greatest tennis match ever played. Others had about the same thing to say as Tilden did—everyone, that is, except Jack Benny. He came in with Lukas and Sullivan, and while they were raving on at length, Benny just shook my hand and mumbled something like "nice match," as if I had won the second round of the mixed doubles at the club. I remember, Jack Benny was the only calm person in the whole locker room. The place was like a madhouse.

Finally, they were all gone and I was able to walk out into the night, out to where all those people still were, milling about their seats. Someone drove me back to the Hurlingham Club, where the team had its meals, but I was too excited to eat. I called my parents, but that only made me more excited still, so I finally just left everyone and took a walk. At last it was getting dark, but I don't remember much except that I left Hurlingham and walked all around Putney Bridge. Later, sometime, I came back and had a bowl of beef soup, and then I fell into bed.

We had to begin to prepare for playing the Challenge Round almost immediately. We managed well enough, I guess, because we beat the British 4-1, which was expected. But I don't think we were actually as well prepared as we might have been if it had not been for the excitement of the Cramm match. I know that I, anyway, could not put that match out of my mind for a long time. Even after we had played and beaten the English, there were still nights when I would wake up in a sweaty nightmare. It was always the same one. It was me behind 4-1 in the fifth set, and Gottfried was looking at me from across the net.

And even after the bad dreams ended, it was still worth speculating about what would have happened had I not pulled the match out. For one very obvious thing, it is likely that if we had not won the Cup but would have had to challenge for it again the next year, 1938, I certainly would not have had the opportunity to try to win the Grand Slam of tennis. I probably would have been too busy working with the team for various preliminary zone matches to concentrate on individual play. Of greater importance, it is even possible to assume that the Germans would have had the Davis Cup when the war broke out and that it would have been in Nazi hands for many years. And if winning the greatest match ever meant the chance for the Grand Slam for me, losing it may have been the first step to jail for Gottfried. Would Hitler have dared to imprison him had Cramm brought the tennis supremacy of the world to the Third Reich?

But it was our team that brought the Davis Cup home to the United States a few weeks later. After I won at Forest Hills I went out to Los Angeles to play in the Pacific Southwest Tournament. After my first-round match there, which was a rather normal, unexciting one, I looked up from my locker, and who should be coming at me but Jack Benny. He was positively beside himself, hardly pausing to say hello before he launched into a babbling, endless dissertation on how wonderful, how exciting, how fantastic the Cramm match had been. It was like one of those scenes from his show. I would keep trying to interrupt him, unsuccessfully. "But Jack——" I would try to start. And he would go right on.

"Magnificent, Don. It was just marvelous. Why when you—— It

was incredible. And then you— Why, I've told everybody about it."
And on he went.

"But Jack—" I kept on, so that at last he stopped long enough
to take that pose he is famous for, the palm cupped on his cheek,
staring at me curiously. "Jack, I don't understand," I began. "At
Wimbledon, after the Cramm match, you were the only person I
met who was relaxed and calm. Now you carry on like this. The
match was two months ago. Then you were unmoved. Now you're
jumping around all excited. What is it?"

"Don," he said. "The truth is, that the Cramm match was the
first tennis I ever saw. Now since then I've seen others, but at the
time I thought all matches were more or less like that." I told him I
was sorry, I would try to do better in the future when he was watching, but that it was a tough act to follow. I never again played in such
a glorious match or had the thrill of coming out of the locker
room and seeing people still standing there, refusing to leave, just
savoring the experience and knowing they would never forget it.

2

I Learn the First Major Rule for Beginners

How I became a tennis champion was, really, a simple matter of using God-given talents to best advantage. That, after all, is the way most winners develop in all sports. But how I came to play tennis at all is another thing altogether. Except for two widely separated events J. Donald Budge would never have hit a tennis ball.

The first incident occurred many years before I was even born. It was a freak accident, the sad misfortune that ended the athletic career of my father, John Budge, but in so doing it set up a chain of events that ended about a quarter of a century later when my older brother humiliated me into picking up a tennis racket. In a way, I was also picking up my father's interrupted career. There is a certain misplaced justice—or irony—in my success, for perhaps it was meant to be realized a generation earlier in another land.

We Budges are Scots. My mother was born in San Francisco, but she was a Pearl Kincaid, so I think that is quite Scottish enough to make me a true Highlander on both sides. In northern Scotland, Budge is, in fact, a commonplace name. I suppose most Budges were content with their homeland, though, for it is rare that I run into another member of the old clan abroad. The one exception was a poor, unknowing naval lieutenant named Donald J. Budge—and I never did meet him. The unlucky fellow was shipped to some obscure island in the Pacific in the middle of the war, and all they wanted to know when he landed was where was his racket and how do you hit a good backhand. Lieutenant Donald J. did not know a backhand from a racket. Lieutenant J. Donald, or me, was still back in the States in the Army Air Force.

My own family came from Wick, Scotland, which even today has a population of hardly 7000. However, by dint of its location, Wick will always possess a certain notoriety far beyond the mere fact of its size. Wick is the northernmost town of any real substance in the British Isles. Beyond Wick there are only the Orkney Islands. The horizon is the Arctic Circle. I have never been to Wick myself, but I think I can say with assurance that very little tennis is played there. In the winter, daylight is only a passing fancy, and all year round the air has a crispness and a dampness that hardly encourage tennis as, say, a warm California sun does.

My father left Wick late in his teens and headed south (that being about the only choice in Wick) to make a living as a professional athlete. Jack Budge, as everyone called him, was an outstanding soccer football player, and Third Lanark, a second-division Scottish football team, signed him on. Dad's only brother was Donald, and he too was a good soccer prospect who also came down into the lowlands to play the game. Besides the two brothers, there were six sisters in the family. My grandfather, the head of the house, was a baker, and a good one.

My father was only about five feet eight inches, but he was quick and agile and gritty, and soon he worked his way up from the Third Lanark team to the Glasgow Rangers, which was—and still is—one of the best first-division teams in the Scottish League. Jack Budge had made the majors. He was only about nineteen or twenty then, and although a lot of athletes burn bright and then fade, there is reason to think that Dad might have eventually enjoyed the equivalent success in football that I subsequently had in tennis.

But such speculation can only be idle, for near the end of practice one wet, murky afternoon, Dad came bursting across after the ball. There was a hard crash as several players from both Ranger squads descended on the ball at once, and in the action, Dad took a brisk kick on his shins and fell down. He knocked his head as he collapsed in the melee, and dropped unconscious. This in itself might not have been a catastrophe, except for a weird stroke of bad luck that greatly compounded the accident.

For at the very instant that Dad crumpled to the ground, the whole action, the flow of the scrimmage, was carried away. Suddenly the ball was down at the other end of the field, the players all chasing after it. Their attention was completely drawn from the action of the previous moment. Then, seconds later, the ball was kicked again, far out of bounds. It had been a long practice, the Rangers were all down by their locker-room entrance now, and someone suggested that this was a good time to quit for the evening. They all hustled off the field. My father, lying still in the dreary pitch of the early Scottish evening, was forgotten and left behind on the ground.

The other players laughed and jostled their way through getting dressed, and it was more than half an hour before my uncle Donald finally noticed that Jack was not there. Even then this was no cause for alarm; Donald's first reaction was probably that Dad had gone on without him. Then, suddenly, Donald had the vague recollection of my father going down in the last moments of the scrimmage. Donald watched that scene cross his mind again and again—Jack going down, Jack going down. But no matter how often he thought about the incident, he couldn't remember Jack getting up. Donald darted out of the locker room, tearing across the field that had already turned dark, to the spot where he found my father, still unconscious and alone where he had been left.

Dad was revived quickly, for though it had been a solid blow, it was not a seriously disabling one. The damage was otherwise. From lying so long on the cold Scottish sod, my father had contracted both pneumonia and bronchitis, infirmities that eventually killed him, although it took forty-five years. He never played athletics again. He just could not breathe well enough. I can remember him now, later in life, when one lung had completely gone and the other was fading too. I can see him, only leaning over to tie his shoe and suddenly catching himself, gasping, trying to breathe the way I might if I had spent a whole strenuous afternoon exerting myself.

His respiratory problems were so immediately obvious after his recovery from the fall that the doctors advised him to leave Scotland for a more beneficial climate. America—California particularly—was suggested, so Dad left Scotland and Wick for good. This was about 1905, and California was a golden land of boom and excitement, but my father was not really looking for fame and fortune, like many others going West. Indeed, if anything, he left his chance for glory on the soccer field that night. Dad came to California just for life.

His first job in the Bay Area was with the San Francisco *Chronicle*, where a Miss Kincaid worked as a linotype operator. Dad had to leave the *Chronicle* after a brief period, for the dirt and closeness of the composing room were too harsh for his lungs, but he did come back to the paper a little while later and retrieved Miss Kincaid. My mother is a wonderful lady, in her eighties now, and still living in the Bay Area, in Walnut Creek. It was my mother who gave me my red head of hair, but my shade is pale beside hers, which, I was told, had been a bright, flaming red. I have to report this on hearsay because I never saw my mother when she had her red hair. On the night of the great San Francisco earthquake, nine years before I was born, Mother's bed was taken up and literally tossed from one side of her room to the other. The experience was so appalling that within ten days Mother's full head of red hair had turned completely white.

Dad left the newspaper for a job driving a laundry truck and eventually moved into the management end of the laundry business. I suppose you can describe us best as a typical middle-class family—not too rich, not too poor. We always had the money to pay our bills on time. We ate well and enjoyed ourselves. I was born at 811 Sixtieth Street in Oakland, but when I was three we moved two blocks to 673 Sixtieth Street, and that was the house that I grew up in. It is still standing, and I visited it the last time I was out there.

It was a sturdy, wooden frame house, with a front porch and a shingle roof. It had two baths and three bedrooms. I shared mine with Lloyd, my brother, who is six years older than I. The other child was Jean, my sister, who was two years older. She is now Mrs. Martin Benson. We made a happy family. I was the baby, of course, the youngest. I was born on June 13, 1915, which is, for a frame of reference, about a month after the *Lusitania* went down. I was named for both my father and his brother, who had stayed behind in Scotland. I was always called by my middle name, though—either Donald or Don.

As a kid, I played and loved all sports. In fact, it is accurate to say that tennis appealed to me the least of all the sports that I was acquainted with. Baseball was my first love, and I can still remember that one of the most pleasant surprises of my life came when I first met Joe DiMaggio. "Don," he said to me, "you know the one thing I always wanted was to be a tennis champion." I had to admit to him that not only had my childhood dream always been to grow up to be a baseball star, but I had even been a center fielder. Joe is hardly six months older than I am, and grew up just across the Bay in the Fisherman's Wharf district. It is the greater coincidence, I think, that we did *not* play against each other in some sport when we were growing up. In fact, I think that after Joe confessed to me that he wanted to be a tennis player and I told him that I had always hoped to be a baseball player, we both sort of stood there, thinking only: There but for the grace of God . . .

Joe was more familiar, however, with the baseball abilities of another tennis player—Alice Marble, my mixed-doubles partner for many years. When he was playing with the old San Francisco Seals of the Pacific Coast League, Alice used to come out before the games at Seals Stadium and shag fly balls during batting practice. DiMaggio told me she had a pretty good arm.

I think fondly of baseball for many reasons, not the least of which is that it was tremendously responsible for my success in tennis, particularly with the backhand, my money shot. I am more or less ambidextrous, even down to my feet—I can punt a football farther left-footed, though I am more accurate kicking with my right foot. My mother was left-handed, and, though I write with my right hand, there are many things I can do better with my left. When I first started playing baseball, I began naturally as a left-handed hitter. It was nothing contrived. Somebody handed me a bat, and I just moved up and took a left-handed stance.

In the same way—just because it felt right—when I later began to play tennis with my brother, Lloyd, I picked up the racket with my right hand. The backhand is almost invariably the hardest shot for a beginner to hit, but for me it was natural and easy. Really, the only difference between a left-handed baseball swing and a right-handed backhand tennis swing is that you use both hands on the baseball bat. And, as a matter of fact, when I was a small beginner, I used both hands to hit a backhand. Even long after I only needed one hand, I was told that a close examination of pictures of myself hitting a backhand could be almost perfectly superimposed over Ted Williams hitting a baseball. I was flattered by the comparison. Another time, a magazine took pictures of me in action and ran them alongside of pictures of Fred Astaire dancing. About the only difference in the poses the camera caught was that I had a racket in my right hand and he had a cane in his . . . and was wearing top hat and tails. I guess tennis put me in pretty good company. The year after I was the personality picked to appear in all the Rheingold Beer advertisements, they started their Miss Rheingold contest. I was the last Mr. Rheingold.

Basketball was another sport that helped my tennis. I was forced to give up baseball when I became serious about tennis, because the seasons conflicted, but I was able to play basketball all the way through high school. I was a forward at University High School in Oakland. I stood all of five feet six and a half (and that half inch was very important to me), but I averaged around eight or ten points a game, and that was pretty good in those days when the scores were a lot lower than they are now. I was also a fantastic free-throw shooter, about ninety per cent accurate, and if that sounds like braggadocio, I apologize, but I think a forward five feet six and a half inches tall is entitled to all the conceit he can muster.

Make no mistake, though, basketball—perhaps even more than baseball—is a sport very complementary to tennis. The movements are quite similar—up and back, cutting, angling, with sharp turns and the need to adjust quickly to a sudden shifting from offense to defense and back again. I am not surprised that a lot of tennis players were also good on the other court. Ellsworth Vines was a great athlete in just about everything he tried, and basketball was one of his best games. Tony Trabert was a fine college basketball player at Cincinnati, and so was Marty Riessen at Northwestern. Of course, if reciprocity was carried to the other extreme, we could, perhaps, get some very interesting results. Can you imagine the angle of serve that would be possible for a seven-footer such as Wilt Chamberlain or Lew Alcindor? It is a rather frightening prospect for those of us who were considered big at six feet one and a half inches.

Football was another sport I loved to play, but I was just too scrawny for that and had to abandon the game fairly early. I can remember fighting the hundred-pound limit for years. I can still see myself now, stuffed and bloated from an average day's accumulation of several meals and more snacks, riding up to the drugstore on my bicycle to weigh in. But always—ninety-seven, ninety-eight, ninety-nine, never a hundred. I could drink ten gallons of water and still be under a hundred. Nothing worked. Still, if I was skinny, I was, on the other hand, short.

I really was five feet six and a half inches all the way through high school. I didn't grow until I was well past my eighteenth birthday. And then—I grew. I shot up like crab grass and exploded almost six inches in a year. The next year I grew another inch and a half and finally crested at six feet one and a half. Growing six inches in a year is not much good, though, unless you are bamboo and nothing is really expected of you in the way of physique. I always weighed less than I should have. During my peak tennis years I never weighed more than 155.

It was no consolation to me at the time, but as it turned out, being small for so long was a distinct advantage for my game. It forced me to learn an entirely different game from the one I would have played had I been a big kid who could just get out on the court and huff and puff and blow everybody down. Since that possibility was denied me, I had to find another way to win; or, rather, I had to find a way *not* to lose. I was really too small to beat anybody. I had to let the big guy across the net beat himself.

The best way to do that was to keep the ball in play. Thus, almost unconsciously, as a matter of survival, I stumbled upon the first major rule for any beginner, of any size or age. Get the ball back into the other person's court. Failing that, just get the ball back. If you just manage that, no matter how atrocious your shot, there is always the chance that your opponent will hit a ball of yours that is going out. And sometimes he will hit the return into the net or out of the court. I know this sounds ridiculously simple, but it is a basic approach that many players ignore. I am forever amazed how many people are surprised when I point out that a 6-4 or 7-5 or any close set is often not the difference of two games, but of one single strategic point.

If you don't believe that, try a bravado sucker ploy. If you play on fairly even terms with someone, agree to give your opponent one extra point that he can declare at his discretion at any spot in the set. That was a game Tilden liked to propose when we were practicing sometimes. He knew if he had that point, he would win a lot more sets. And I guarantee you if you give your close competitor the same advantage, he will turn a close series into a rout in his favor, even though all your scores might be 6-4. Only, you'll invariably be the four.

Getting the ball back will, in the long run, give you the same advantage as that built-in "gimme" point, for if you manage to get enough bad shots back your opponent is eventually bound to miss a return. And this is not just a strategy for a beginner or for someone disadvantaged, as I was by my size. A surprising number of very good players have used it to carry them a long way. The best example I can think of is Whitney Reed, who was a world-class player a few years ago. Whitney had a good backhand as a base to a collection of otherwise undistinguished strokes, but he was a terrific competitor and as good a scrambler as I have ever seen. Talk about getting the ball back! Whitney would kick it back, butt it back, bounce it back, dribble it back, tease it back, laugh it back. Occasionally he would even hit it back, and I don't mean that disparagingly, but as a genuine compliment. Whitney Reed did get the ball back, although he frequently ended up after a point sitting on his rear or sprawled out on his chest. But more often than not his exasperated opponent would then miss the shot, and Whitney would get up off the ground and start getting the ball back all over again.

Unfortunately, one morning he woke up and found out that he had been ranked as the number-one player in the United States. It was the worst thing that could possibly have happened, for suddenly Whitney got the idea that if he were number one, then he must live up to the image and play like Jack Kramer or someone like that. So Whitney began playing in the classic Jack Kramer style, and, regrettably, like so many others, Whitney Reed was not Jack Kramer. His new classic strokes were certainly more esthetically appealing than the old Whitney Reed swings and stabs, and he was on his feet after every point, but he was also losing most of them.

Usually, however, the major force that works against the simple strategy of getting the ball back is the determination of most young players to murder every shot. I suppose this is primarily the result of our times, and particularly of the privilege we all enjoy of being able to see great athletes in action so regularly. We appreciate, so we try to emulate. I'm sure that if we had had television when I was growing up, and I had watched Ellie Vines a few times, then maybe little ninety-eight-pound weakling Don Budge would have tried to hit all his shots like Vines.

Luckily, however, since I didn't know how Vines or anybody else hit the ball, I just got in there and swung my way, returned the ball, and cut down a lot of sluggers. But nowadays every Little Leaguer tries to hit a 380-foot home run, just like Willie Mays, and tries to throw a pinpoint 65-yard touchdown pass, just like Johnny Unitas, and tries to ace in a 115-m.p.h. serve, just like Rod Laver—and tries to do these things every time. I think a lot of kids are inhibiting their own development by accelerating their pace.

Too many youngsters starting in with tennis are really playing handball. They refuse to let the racket do the work it was designed for. They clobber every ball that comes their way, and follow through with a violent enthusiasm that succeeds only in smothering the shot. A follow-through is essential to a good groundstroke, of course. You should not stop the swing as soon as you have hit the ball, as if your racket has just struck a stone wall. But in emphasizing the importance of the follow-through I think perhaps we have too often succeeded only in emphasizing the extent of it.

A good follow-through is like a good handshake, firm but moderate. The bone-rattling handshake is no more pleasing than the flabby paw. Similarly, the roundhouse convoluted follow-through is really no improvement over no follow-through. It destroys accuracy and disturbs balance. I would suggest that your follow-through should extend to an imaginary line, which, if drawn out, would lead straight to the point where you want your shot to land. The best way to find this groove is to stand on the court and actually pretend that you are going to release your racket after the shot so that it would sail directly after the ball. For a simple analogy, keep in mind that in baseball, it is only the powerhouse pull hitter who swings from the heels with a sweeping follow-through. The capable singles hitter, who is looking for the spot—which is the case in tennis—controls his swing so that he can control the ball.

I would never have given up a baseball bat for a tennis racket, I am sure, had it not been for the persistence of my older brother, Lloyd. He dragged me onto a court for the first time when I was thirteen, and thereafter he would take me out there whenever he was desperate for someone to hit with. Lloyd was a good player—he played number one on the University of California team and reached number two in the Northern California sectional rankings —and he truly adored the game, though he was also a fine baseball and basketball player. Lloyd later became a teaching pro and has since stayed in tennis in the court-construction business. He is not quite as tall as I am, but we share a definite resemblance and are often mistaken for each other.

I certainly was not much competition for him in Oakland. Not only was he much older than I, but he also had matured and grown at an earlier age than I was then, so that Lloyd had developed a hard, tough man's game when he was still a teen-ager. He also was aware that I didn't really care for the game, but he found out that I did have one saving grace: I could get the ball back.

So when Lloyd needed practice and could find no one else, he would hunt me down, hand me one of his old rackets, and take me out to Bushrod Park to utilize me as a human backboard. Bushrod Park was two blocks from home, a good public park with two hardball fields, softball diamonds, basketball courts, swings and jungle gyms, and three gravel courts. It was there that I was to learn the game. The gravel was slippery and hard on the balls. The lime on the court lines would come off on the balls, and they would carry it to the racket, and it would eat through the strings in record time. But since I had never been to Newport, it was fine with me. When I really got involved with the game a few years later, there were times when I was at the Bushrod courts literally at sunup.

Still, the first couple of years that I played I don't suppose that Lloyd got me on the courts more than ten or fifteen times a year, and that is really an insignificant amount of practice in California, where you could play practically every day. I thought very little about the game. Getting the ball back was not so much grand strategy on my part as it was a way of making sure that I did not have to chase down too many balls.

My scuffling tactics were somehow appreciated by Lloyd, however, for one night, two or three weeks before my fifteenth birthday, in May of 1930, he started the dinner-table conversation by declaring that he believed I could win the upcoming California State fifteen-and-under championships. My first reaction to this, I think, was little more than a so-what shrug. But Lloyd accepted my smugness in stride and began to pay me back, taunting me, razzing me, and generally embarrassing me in front of the whole family. In a word, he was calling me lazy. I leapt at his bait, and agreed to enter. I would show him—which, of course, is exactly what Lloyd had hoped for. My father also agreed to make the ante a more practical one and promised to buy me some tennis clothes, if I won the first-round match. He was hedging his bet because he still wasn't sure that this wasn't just a friendly brotherly quarrel, and he certainly had no intention of spending good money to outfit me in a sport that would turn out to be just a passing fancy.

But I really was determined, and in the two weeks that remained before the tournament began, I worked diligently, every day, at what was, for all practical purposes, a new game to me. A new challenge, at any rate. I would hit with Lloyd or anybody *I* could shanghai onto the courts, or if I had to, I would just bang a ball up against the board by myself. By the time the tournament began, I possessed two impressive facilities: the baseball backhand and an ability to run all day. My deficiencies were more apparent and more numerous. Most of my strokes were spotty. I was too small to serve with any real power. I had no conception whatsoever of a net game. My idea of tactics incorporated about as much strategy as fills the head of the average Chesapeake Bay retriever in pursuit of a downed mallard. Get it back. But then, truthfully, the game I had going into my first tournament was essentially, and with only slight refinements, the same one I used to win the National Juniors three years later. Only after I grew did my game really mature.

My opponent in the first round—and I still remember his name—was Phil Carlin. He was, coincidentally, also the number-one seed, but this fact could not disturb me as the only seeds I knew about were Burpee. But *I* may have unnerved Phil Carlin, for here I arrived, this redheaded urchin in dirty sneakers, a plain white T-shirt and a pair of light-tan corduroy trousers that were the nearest approximation to tennis whites that we could uncover in my wardrobe. The corduroy was heavy, of course, particularly as I was dashing around under the hot sun, but it never even occurred to me to speculate on this disadvantage. I just chased all over the court and hit my baseball backhand as if it were a man on first and hit-and-run, and before either Phil Carlin or I knew what had happened, I had won the match in two pretty easy straight sets.

Immediately everybody was there raving over me, congratulating me for beating Phil Carlin. Of course, to me, who I had beaten was of little importance. I just scampered away as quickly as I could and called home with the good news. I had won the first round! The very next day, true to their promise, my parents took me into downtown Oakland and bought me a pair of real white ducks and some tennis shirts. No player, professional or amateur, has ever been more happily rewarded. I went on to win the tournament too—just as Lloyd had predicted—and in more appropriate sartorial style. The funny thing is, though, that I never really ever had a racket of my own. I continued to use Lloyd's hand-me-downs until finally Wilson put me on their "free list."

While my first tournament was hardly enough to turn me into an overnight sensation, it certainly did change my thinking about tennis. I was, first of all, immensely proud of the accomplishment. The trophy for the tournament had been displayed in a downtown store window, and as I moved nearer to the finals, I would spend more time, regularly, in front of that window, gazing fondly at the trophy. When I did win it, when that marvelously handsome reward was truly all mine, I could not contain myself. I could not have it just *sit* there in the house. Surely, not enough spectator traffic. So I tucked it under one arm, and beginning right next door at 675 Sixtieth, I trooped the neighborhood, knocking on the doors of people we knew and showing them the first fruits of my tennis victory.

I began to concentrate more on the game too, and sometimes I can remember arriving at Bushrod at dawn before the little old Italian gentleman who was in charge of lining and dragging the gravel. My new attentions toward tennis made baseball suffer the most, but even in that first flush of victory I was still able to be very analytical. I looked at things objectively, and decided I could get further in tennis than in baseball. Indeed, as soon as the California State was over, I began to make long-range plans for someday winning the National Junior title. There was certainly a large element of teen-age daydream involved, but much of my thinking was really a cool, hardheaded projection of the possibilities as I saw them.

Of course, at the time I had no realistic measure of my talents. Some great players had come out of the San Francisco-Oakland area—Little Billy Johnston, Alice Marble, Helen Wills, and Helen Jacobs—but my own competition remained among those rather unknown quantities who, like myself, would show up, eager and anonymous, to play in the turkey tournaments that were held at Golden Gate Park across the Bay. Golden Gate, with its modern asphalt courts, was a marvel to me. It was years before Bushrod's gravel was covered over.

The one testing match that I did have that first summer was with Frankie Parker, the "Boy Wonder" of tennis, when he came out to play in the California Juniors at the Berkeley Tennis Club. Parker was only fourteen, about six months younger than myself, and everybody was already touting him as the great player of the future. I was, naturally, a bit jealous of the hot-shot kid and of all the publicity he was already receiving, but I found it impossible to hold his celebrity against him once I got to meet him. Unlike most child stars, who tend to be self-centered spoiled brats, Frankie was quiet and unassuming, a model of the perfect gentleman I always found him. Indeed, his early success was largely due to his amenable behavior, for he was eminently coachable, a young boy who took suggestion well. He picked things up very quickly, for he was agreeable to following advice and he was, too, simply a wonderfully well-coordinated athlete, someone who could have played any sport well.

Parker drew me in an early round and his coach, Mercer Beasley, who traveled with Frankie, rated me as such an unlikely threat to the Boy Wonder that even before our match started he left and wandered off to scout Parker's *next* opponent. With Beasley away, I beat Frankie in the first set and went ahead of him 3-1 in the second—and this was best of three. At about this time, however, the news of the impending upset worked its way back to Beasley, and he scurried back.

He stood there on the side of the court and just studied me for a few minutes. Then he called Frankie over between games and whispered something in his ear. I was rather bemused, delighted with all the attention I was receiving. We had drawn a good gallery too. But then we went back to play, and immediately, all Parker hit me was an alternate succession of drop shots and lobs—back, up, back, up. It was the perfect tactic, since I still had no net game whatsoever and little better idea of how to cope with a lob. I knew that myself. The only thing that annoyed me was that Parker hadn't been smart enough to figure it out, and needed his coach to do his thinking. But coach and player together were too much for me. As soon as the new strategy was installed, Parker swept me to a snappy defeat, and from there the Boy Wonder went on to new horizons. I went back to Oakland.

My first trip of any sort was to Los Angeles, for a state junior round-robin tournament down there. I felt excited and, under the circumstances of my first trip, a bit adventurous. I won my first match rather impressively too, and as I came off the court there was Perry Jones waiting for me. Even then he was the head of southern California tennis. He beckoned me to him and I hustled right over to pick up a compliment. Instead, with a distinct frown, he looked me up and down. "Budge," Mr. Jones finally snarled, "those are the dirtiest tennis shoes I ever saw in my life. Don't you ever—don't you *ever*—show up again on any court anywhere at any time wearing shoes like that." That was all the compliments he seemed to be dispensing this day, so I nodded and slunk off, properly chastened. Perry hasn't changed his demands much over the years, either. I read just recently that he told some of his juniors to get their hair cut or not to bother to come back for their next match. I know he made an impression on me, for I've never gone on court since that day with even scuffy shoes.

Certainly I was also very aware of the new surroundings and the elite social company that I had been thrust into. But if I was aware, I was not self-conscious about my entrance into the strange world of country-club life. It is unfortunate in many ways that tennis is still much the domain of the rich. It is more regrettable, though, that the sport is still saddled with an image of snobbery that is not altogether fair. Even in the early thirties, when I was breaking in, tennis was becoming more than a rich man's diversion.

I was accepted and certainly had no barriers to hurdle, for other public-park players had come to exert a strong influence on tennis in the decade before I began to play. George Lott and John Doeg had been players, like myself, who had come from modest circumstances, and Ellsworth Vines, another public-courts graduate, had succeeded them to prominence. I was never once made uncomfortable by the wealthy people who sponsored the tournaments and dominated most of the tennis hierarchy.

The next summer, when I was seventeen, the Northern California Tennis Association sent me on a more extended tour into the Northwest. I played in tournaments in Portland and Seattle and even across the border into Vancouver. I won the Western Canadian Juniors there for my first international title. I had more difficulty in the big tournaments back in California, for Charles Hunt, whose younger brother Joe won the Nationals in 1943, was a year older than me and my constant nemesis. He had a hard serve, with a big hop—something like Von Cramm's, I suppose you can say—and he was forever beating me. Then, the next year, when Hunt graduated from the juniors, it was Gene Mako, another Californian, who was later to be my regular doubles partner and great friend, whom everyone rated as the comer.

When I went East in 1933 for the first time, the summer I was eighteen, Mako was seeded first in the National Juniors, while I was neither seeded nor ranked nationally. Parker was by now the biggest hotshot of all in the juniors, but the Boy Wonder, at seventeen, already considered himself too advanced for junior play. He did not even deign to show up for the Nationals, which were held at the Culver Military Academy in Indiana. Instead he stayed on the eastern grass-court circuit, where he could play against the men.

So Parker was not there, and despite being unseeded, I was placed in the other half of the draw from Mako and won my way to the finals against him. I was still only five feet six and a half, still just a tireless little retriever without a serve, and I went right out and won the first two sets from Mako. But then I reversed my field, lost the next two 1-6 and 0-6 and fell behind 3-5 in the deciding set. He was serving for the match when I broke him. Then I went on to win the championship 8-6.

A few weeks later I read an article by Bill Tilden. He wrote, "The future of American tennis rests with Gene Mako, Frank Parker, and possibly Don Budge." Boy, did that make me mad. I was infuriated. *I* was the champion, and still *I* was the "possibly." But also, at last, I was growing. I was growing right out of my skin, out of the little-man's game of getting it back, into a new role where I not only could get the ball back but could dare an opponent to try to do the same.

3

Grass and Other Vicissitudes

Once I had won the Juniors and was able to appreciate fully the opportunity that I had in tennis, I elevated the sport to a position in my thinking that superseded every other interest. In taking anything under consideration, I examined it first from one single viewpoint: Is this good for my tennis, or is it not?

Not all choices, of course, meant a total sacrifice in the name of tennis. I did not drink or smoke in the first place, so there was nothing in the way of temptation involved there; but, as it turned out rather disastrously, I did not give up sweets sufficiently. There were times, though, when I had to be most determined to maintain the discipline I had set for myself—turning into a pumpkin at midnight at some dance or party, or passing up invitations altogether. Tennis also caused me to drop out of college, although the decision was not meant to be a final one.

In the spring of 1934—my freshman year at the University of California—the chance came for me to join the Davis Cup auxiliary team. Here was an opportunity to travel abroad and see the world, and I just could not afford to pass it up. I would return to Berkeley the next fall, back on my way to a diploma and an honest nine-to-five job after that. As it turned out, though, things just kept tumbling over each other, and I never did make it back to Cal. On the other hand, there has never been much time in my life since then that I have been far away from tennis.

That summer of '34, I made it all the way to the East Coast grass circuit. I had had one brief experience with grass a few years before in British Columbia, but this was my first prolonged association with turf—the painful beginning of a grueling relationship. I don't like grass any better now than I did then, but neither do almost all the good players who have had great success on grass. Gonzales, Kramer, Riggs, Laver, and just about everybody else of that caliber would like to see it weeded out of tennis altogether, once and for all time.

Grass is a charming enough idea, of course. It is pretty and it smells nice, and it is pleasant to run around on out there in the green outdoors. But these rather tenuous reasons aside, it is difficult to find any more substantial evidence in the defense of grass. The best players win on grass. The best players would win on bubble gum. But the ragged inconsistency of the grass surface makes the game less fun and of lower caliber. It is like putting a good football team on a muddy field.

Still, although virtually none of the best players likes to play on grass, it remains the surface upon which most all of the world's most important matches are contested. It is all a matter of tradition, I suppose. Games like court tennis, which was originally played in a courtyard, were devised centuries ago, but the tennis we know—*lawn* tennis—was introduced, on grass, to England in 1873 by Walter C. Wingfield. The first courts were on grass, and the major courts have remained of grass even if virtually no others in the world have that surface.

With regard to grass, you seem to hear most of all that it is a fast surface. This is true, but only to a point. Grass is certainly faster than clay, but it is a great deal slower than hardwood or canvas, the two surfaces we used almost exclusively in the pros. Manuel Santana won the Wimbledon title on grass, but now he even refuses to play on the hard indoor surfaces because he feels they are so fast that the whole game becomes mostly serve and volley.

So speed is not the major identifying characteristic of grass. What is, is the bad bounce. It is just too difficult to keep any ground perfectly level and the grass alive and even. The needs of a grass court have invariably turned out to be much too demanding.

Indeed, except at Wimbledon, this is universally so. In all the matches that I played at Wimbledon—and there are a lot of courts at Wimbledon—I don't believe I received more than a total of four bad bounces. But on any other grass court, from Forest Hills to White City, to Orange, to Queens, to Newport, I don't believe I ever finished a single *set* without at least four bad bounces. Wimbledon is like a divine intervention and is really not germane to the issue.

All other grass courts drive you to distraction. Moving onto grass was particularly difficult for me, coming directly from a lifetime of playing on the smooth California cement courts. Californians are spoiled by a game where the ball always bounces true, right into your racket. You can expect it. Suddenly, thrown on grass, you are faced with a steady succession of bizarre bounces, and your whole routine and confidence are undermined.

Besides, a ball skids off grass more than it bounces, so that even when I got a fair bounce, it was not the nice fat California hop I had been used to. You must learn to bend much lower to hit your groundstrokes. It is only the difference of a few inches, but the change was substantial enough to force me to alter my forehand from a western grip to an eastern grip after that first summer.

I was also unprepared for the need to get to the net as quickly as possible during my first season of grass play. I had grown to a point where I was big enough and physically capable of managing a good net game, but I had not learned the subtleties or confidence of net play, so I wasn't naturally inclined to rush in as I should have done, and later did. On grass you must follow behind your first fair shot in a rush for the net. On clay, if you try to come in on anything less than a good shot, you'll be slipping and sliding in the middle of the court at about the time that your opponent sends a passing shot by you.

It is my own feeling that tennis needs a universal surface and that the best such surface would be asphalt or cement. I'm sure that I will promptly be accused of being a provincial old Californian who can't see past the Sierra Mountains, but I have played on a lot of different surfaces under the most fascinating range of conditions, and cement is best. It is a hard, fast surface that provides the quick action that most players and spectators prefer. It is easy to maintain and as level as a freeway, so the ball bounces fast and true. The player can concentrate on playing the game instead of the bounces.

The major criticism of cement courts is that they force blisters. And at times they do. It was always my experience, however, that it was not the *type* of court that caused blisters but the *change* in courts. Any change. That first summer that I went East from cement *to* grass, I came up with some of the dandiest blisters that I ever was to develop in my entire career. And many other players have had the same experience.

It is really ridiculous when you consider all the geographical and political distinctions that prevail in what is one of the simplest games that has ever been devised. Not only are players forced to endure a change in surface about every time they cross a boundary line, but the difference in the balls thmselves can be just as significant. Generally, Slazenger balls are used in Europe, Wilson or Spalding in the United States. Because the Slazenger ball is so much faster than either of the American models, I always found it foolish to try to make an immediate adjustment from one to the other. It was my custom, and that of most of my contemporaries, to take our first week back in the United States playing doubles only. That gave us time to lose our sea legs and get properly reacquainted with the new balls and the typical bad bounces.

If we weren't playing, we practiced. That was our leisure. A movie was an occasion. I hear all these stories nowadays about amateur tennis circuits being bacchanalian exercises for heavily bankrolled players, rich with phony expense money, and they certainly are interesting revelations for me. I was provided with exactly three dollars a week for meals and a buck and a half each week for laundry. Even at my peak as an amateur, if I was able to manage to save a couple hundred dollars out of a year's expense money, I considered myself not only thrifty, but extravagantly well off as well.

But money, which was scarce enough anyway those years, was only of passing interest to me. I was like a kid who had run away with the circus. It was totally new and exciting. I was developing my game and the first touches of a reputation as well. In the National

Clay Courts, which most of the big-name players skipped, I lasted
all the way to the finals before Bitsy Grant beat me. I got to Bitsy
and the finals by coming past Frankie Parker in the semis, and there
was a special satisfaction in that, for I hadn't faced the Boy Wonder since that lobbing match four years before.

This time, it was I who came from behind: 2-6, 3-6, 6-3, 6-0,
9-7. It was an unmercifully hot day in Chicago, as muggy and sear-
ing, perhaps, as I ever was to find the weather. I was almost with-
ered by the end, and Frankie suffered cramps. It is usually also
written that he played with a bloody nose, suggesting, perhaps,
that we were really slugging it out. Actually what happened was that
while we were changing over one time, Parker's nose itched and he
scratched it with his racket. Somehow, the end of the racket clipped
a bit of the skin, and drew about one c.c. of blood. When he wiped
his nose on the towel, it was wired around the world that Parker
and Budge had engaged in a bloody dog fight.

At Forest Hills in September I lasted to the fourth round—the
round of 16—before I was beaten by Vernon Kirby, who was a
pretty fair South African player and certainly no disgrace to lose to.
Perhaps even more heartening than this or even the Clay Courts,
however, was my first meeting with Fred Perry, the world's ranking
player. It came at Berkeley in the Pacific Coast Championships, a
few weeks after Forest Hills. This was my territory and my surface,
of course, but I carried Fred the maximum of five sets before he
beat me 7-5 in the fifth. That was a glorious way to end my first
season, whatever the circumstances.

I had a chance to go play in South America or along the Riviera
that winter, but I decided that it was more important for me to stay
home in the more prosaic world of Alameda County and practice
with Tom Stow. He was really the only coach I ever had. He had
been a good player, winner of the intercollegiate doubles title, but
he was never a great one. Stow was, however, a clever tennis tech-
nician. He knew the game. He was pro at the Claremont Country
Club in Oakland then, and is still active, now at the Silverado Country Club in Napa, California. Tom approached me after I won the
Juniors, and offered to work with me. His payment, he knew, had

to come from satisfaction and faith. Since I could hardly afford to pay for such professional coaching, Tom knew that his reward could only derive from the publicity he would receive for being my coach *if* I became a big name. It turned out, of course, to be a good deal for us both, and one year I was even able to nominate Tom as Davis Cup coach. He was selected.

That fall of '34 we agreed it was necssary to change my forehand grip, and that was our first project. I also needed a great deal of work in learning to play the net and in how to force the action. Tom and I worked well together. By the end of the winter my game had clearly improved, particularly as I had mastered the eastern grip. I advise this grip for almost all players because it seems to me to be the grip that has proved to be the best for hitting balls at all the various levels.

As I said, the western grip was best only if you were playing on California cement, where the bounces set up nice and high. The player with the western grip who was best able to get low bounces on all surfaces was Little Bill Johnston, and he managed not so much because of the grip but because he was small enough to get his whole body down after low balls.

There are exceptions, then, and occasionally I will come across an inexperienced player who hits well despite an unorthodox grip. My feeling then is that the player should keep his grip, however much it conflicts with esthetics and custom. Françoise Durr, the 1967 French champion, has her own special grip that virtually defies analysis, but she hits the ball almost as well as any woman in the world, and it would be foolhardy, I think, for any coach to try to get her to change her style.

For the average player, though, I would suggest the simple eastern grip for the forehand. It is sometimes called the shake-hands grip. Just remember that. The flat part of your hand should go onto the flat part of the racket handle. In essence, the racket becomes an extension of your hand.

Besides working to perfect the new grip, I had also spent much time in conditioning. I was stronger than ever, and as it turned out this was immediately important, because my first stop that spring

of '35 was Davis Cup play in Mexico City, where the air is so
sparse you can practically see what splotches of oxygen there are,
floating about in the empty space.

We went to Mexico to play not only the host team but the Chinese as well, whom we had to meet first. These were American Zone
matches, the winner to eventually play the European Zone winner
for the right to challenge the defending champion. The Davis Cup
is the only major competition in any sport where the defender is
given a free ride to the finals, or, truly, "The Challenge Round."

The competition began in 1900 when Dwight F. Davis donated
a cup that the Americans and the English battled for. Other countries began to join in, though, and eventually it was necessary to
break the early-round challengers into geographical groupings.
When I played there were just the European and American Zones.
Now there are four, the European having been divided into two distinct groups, and an Asian Zone has also been added. The Cup has
never been too strict about geography, though. Brazil, for instance,
traditionally plays in one of the European zones, and there we were
in Mexico City to play China in the opening round of the American
Zone. The winner would earn the right to meet the host team afterwards.

Our squad was captained by Walter Pate, and it included Bitsy
Grant and me for the singles, and Gene Mako, who had begun to
team with me the year before, to play in the doubles. Neither the
Chinese nor the Mexicans had been figured to provide the United
States with much competition, so Grant, Mako, and I were selected
instead of the older regulars—Sidney Wood, Wilmer Allison, and
John Van Ryn. It was primarily supposed to be a good experience
for the younger players, which it was, but I don't think anyone seriously envisioned that any of us would compete in the more important matches later in the season. We were supposed to still be too
young.

We first beat China 5-0, and followed that up by clinching over
Mexico 3-0. There were still the last day's two singles matches that
had to be played as a formality, so Mako came to visit Captain Pate

and asked him if it would be possible for him to be substituted for Bitsy or myself in one of the remaining matches. "After all this time down here," Gene said, "I'd just like to play one singles." Pate agreed and got the Mexican captain to also give his permission— which is necessary in a case such as this—so after I won my match the next day to make the score 4-0, Gene took the court against Esteban Reyes, the number-one player in Mexico.

It was a hotter, thinner day than even Mexico City is normally accustomed to, and by the time Mako and Reyes hit the court, the oxygen must have been hiding in the shade. We were playing in Chapultepec, the major Mexico City tennis arena, and the center court is surrounded on all sides by seats and walls, so that it can be a stifling enclosure. But it is a roomy court. The surface is a dusty brick-red clay, and it covers a large territory, deep and wide beyond the lined court itself. In fact, so far back did the area behind the court extend that the groundskeepers had not even bothered to remove some of their tools and a wheelbarrow. They remained there, right at the foot of the back wall, many yards behind the baseline.

Gene, gasping, broke even with Reyes in the first two sets, but the Mexican pulled away in the third set and soon had Gene at set point. Reyes served, he and Gene exchanged shots, and then Reyes clipped the ball just over the net. Mako came puffing in, and barely managed to push the shot back. Gene just stood there, glassy-eyed, at the net. Reyes took the return and lifted a high, deep lob. Boom —it landed right inside the baseline and bounced far away. Mako stumbled after it, caught the lob on the bounce, and sent a shot back to Reyes.

Reyes promptly drop-shotted again, and here came Mako weaving back to the net to save it. Somehow he did catch up with the ball and returned it. Reyes lobbed it right back. Boom. Mako staggered after it, somehow chased down the lob, and with a final, desperate effort he returned the ball to Reyes. By now, though, Gene was far back behind the baseline, giddy with the air and practically out of control. He took one more uncertain step, tripped, and toppled flat out into the wheelbarrow on his back, his legs and arms draped out over the sides. Reyes casually plopped the return back into the court to finish off the set and take a 2-1 lead at the rest period.

Mako remained in a heap. The red clay that had been left in the wheelbarrow was by now caked all over him, from head to where his knees stuck up. In those days we were still wearing long white gabardine trousers, and Gene's were simply splattered red with Chapultepec clay.

He remained immobile in the wheelbarrow, breathing desperately, gasping more at the thought of the hundred-yard walk he now had to take to reach the locker room. Finally, a sympathetic workman was no longer able to ignore Gene's sad plight. The man came over, grasped the wheelbarrow handles, and began to steer Mako down the side of the court, off to the locker room. Gene was so tired and dirty, he not only failed to protest the transportation but also defaulted the whole match. Bitsy and I were in hysterics at the whole scene. And that was the way my first Davis Cup experience ended—watching my proud American teammate and Davis Cup doubles partner being carted out of the stadium in a wheelbarrow, gasping for breath and colored red like a giant chili pepper.

In great contrast, my next Davis Cup match, hardly two months later, began in dead earnestness, with me playing the opening match for the United States in a match against a major opponent and a major tennis nation on the Centre Court of Wimbledon. My arrival to this position had been swift and surprising, even to myself, and the decision to play me in this Interzone Final against Germany was made only a couple of days before I took the court against Henner Henkel. I was still officially the number-nine American player, but I had beaten both Wood and Allison, the two top-ranked players, in practice matches, so at last the decision was made to go with me and bench Wood.

I was naturally nervous when I went out to play Henkel, but in a sense I was lucky. Of all the world-class players at the time, Henkel may have been the best opponent that I could have drawn for my main-event Davis Cup debut. He was a solid, sturdy six-footer who managed to hit a powerful cannonball serve with a backswing that he could uncoil easily within the walls of a phone booth. He just drew that racket back a few inches and then brought it forward with all the power of a slingshot. He was probably the strongest tennis player I ever knew, and certainly the one with the most incredible appetite. Henkel was one of those fellows who could eat two or three dozen oysters at a quick sitting, for I saw him do just that several times in Australia. Indeed, watching Henkel eat was one of the more interesting spectator diversions in my life, for his appetite was not only prodigious but exotic as well. The juxtaposition of his entrees was often more spectacular than the size or number of them. You know, he was the sort who would start off a meal with a chocolate sundae, follow that with a few mouthfuls of spaghetti, and then move on to something really interesting and substantial.

As strong as he was, though, his first serve was not as reliable as his stomach, and his second serve was a little cream puff. It was, at times, hard to believe that a man of such strength and with such a hard first serve could hit such a dainty little second serve. When Henkel's first serve was on, he was virtually unbeatable. When it was not, the weak second serve made his whole game vulnerable. A more consistent player would certainly have been a much tougher type for a rookie to face in his major opening assignment.

True to his usual form, too, Henkel was not able to maintain great service against me. He also missed opportunities to capitalize on my mistakes, and I edged him in both the first two sets, 7-5 and 11-9. He came back to take me in the third set, 8-6, but in the fourth, his first serve deserted him more than before, and I launched into an attack on the weak second serve. I won 6-1 for the match and the first American point.

Cramm beat Allison in straight sets to end the first day's play in a tie, and the Germans were in a favored position entering the doubles against Allison and Van Ryn. Cramm was partnered with Kay Lund, and they took a 2-1 lead in sets. The Americans were then somehow able to pull it out 9-7 and 8-6, but only after facing down five match points. One of them was the occasion when Lund returned what appeared to be the winning shot—and it would have been had not Cramm volunteered the admission that the ball had

ticked his racket before Lund hit it. The Germans would have almost surely taken the Interzone championship had Cramm com-
promised his honor.

As it was, the close, emotional doubles loss probably took some
heart out of the Germans, and surely Cramm was terribly dejected
by the time we met in the last match, for by then Allison
had trounced Henkel to clinch the victory for us. Our match was
meaningless, then, so that I have never felt that it was really a genuine win on my part. Cramm took the first set from me at love, and
having proved what he could do, he seemed to lose all interest in the
proceedings, and I won the next three sets over his listless opposition. It counted for nothing, of course, but I think Gottfried may
have hurt himself in the long run by giving me the chance to beat
him. He had defeated me soundly at Wimbledon a short time before, and I had no faith at all that I could beat him. It was he who
opened the door for my hope, because once you have beaten someone, no matter how tainted the win, it is a great deal easier to accomplish it the next time.

The same thing happened to me the next year after Australia
eliminated us from the Davis Cup. We scheduled some exhibitions
with England, and in one, at Eastbourne, I whipped Perry in four
sets. Again, it was a situation where I was playing to win, while he
was playing for exercise, but just the fact of the win gave me a confidence that heretofore I had not dared to express. I believe too
that the insignificant victory at Eastbourne was directly responsible
for my almost beating Perry a few months later at Forest Hills. A
match may be meaningless in one context but quite significant in
others.

The only time I had played Cramm prior to this Davis Cup match
had been at Wimbledon a few weeks before. He had routed me in
the semifinals, 4-6, 6-4, 6-3, 6-2, and the scores are particularly
telling because they suggest what in fact happened: The longer we
played, the more he dominated me. But I was not discouraged by
my performance. It was at least educational—learning at the feet
of a master under the most exacting circumstances. Also, I was so
thrilled and pleased to have lasted to the semis that it would have

required an exceptionally embarrassing loss to have shattered that euphoria completely.

A player does not necessarily need a great success in his first year at Wimbledon to satisfy himself. The tournament is so wonderful just in itself that victories become almost superfluous. You don't have to catch the brass ring the first time on a carousel; you don't have to fall in love at your first dance. Being at Wimbledon is a warm enough novelty itself.

I am also delighted that the tournament's style has not changed a whit since I played there. But then, as any player would swear, to tamper with Wimbledon would be to tinker with perfection. The tournament captures the best of all worlds. It has *élan* and grace. And it is also efficient. If you are a few minutes late for a match, don't bother; you have already been defaulted. You are given four minutes to warm up before a match. Four minutes means 240 seconds. Things move with that dispatch throughout the entire two weeks, and if the attitude seems too harsh, you have not experienced the chaos that ensues at most tournaments as soon as a rule is bent just a little for pleasantry's sake. Wimbledon's machine-gun operation is welcomed by the players.

And the players are welcomed in turn. Rolls Royce or Daimler limousines are put at the players' beck and call, from the champion right down to number 128 in the men's draw. The players are feted, dined, cared for, loved. Their every whim is answered. And above all, the response that impressed me most when I arrived for my first Wimbledon was just that we were noticed. In the United States and in many other countries, even at the peak of my fame, I could appear almost anywhere without being recognized. In London, almost from the first, when I was the ninth-ranked American player, from Oakland, California, I was a celebrity, just as all players at Wimbledon are celebrities. I can still recall the tingling thrill of having someone recognize me when I was merely riding out on the underground to the Queen's Club to practice.

The truth is, as corny as it sounds, that even the most experienced athlete (in any sport) plays better when he is appreciated. At Wimbledon, where every seat is sold months in advance, where scalpers do a land-office business, and where the crowds sleep in line the night before good matches to ensure themselves the few standing-room tickets, a tennis player feels . . . well, I guess we feel like a baseball or football player. In those days, when there was no television to cover the scene, there were many people who would buy a ticket for several shillings that only permitted them on the grounds. These fans could not get into the enclosed stadiums to see any of the important matches, but all they wanted was to have a vantage point where they could keep up with the action on the electric scoreboards. The ticket demand is such now that a lottery must be held each year and the tickets distributed that way.

When you are surrounded by this sort of affection and attention, you can imagine that the competitors would just naturally play harder—out of gratitude—even if Wimbledon were anything less than the world's championship.

The British are all such excellent tennis experts that a player's game has to rise simply as a matter of self-defense. The British fans are critics, but they are as fair as they are knowledgeable, and playing at Wimbledon is much like an appearance before a jury.

Can you imagine anything more embarrassing, for instance, than playing Centre Court with a substantial defect in your game? If you have, say, a bad second serve, you can be sure that this point has been carefully aired in the papers for days, that it has been pub and dinner-table conversation as well, and that when you step on the court, every single one of the 18,000 people in attendance *knows* you have a bad second serve, knows exactly what is wrong with your second serve, and is waiting to see how your opponent goes about annihilating your second serve. So you stand out there, naked, before 18,000 expert judges, and you are determined not to show a bad second serve. At Wimbledon people don't cheer or yell so much as they nod. They know full well what to expect.

But beyond all this, there is one last special blessing that Wimbledom reserves only for the players. The courts are magnificent. They manage to combine all that is glorious about the spirit of grass with the sheer functional advantage of the man-made surface. The result is that you not only get good bounces, but you get good bounces on lovely courts. The Wimbledon courts are certainly helped by the wet, dreary climate that keeps the grass lush and thick, but it is not just the environment that is responsible for the courts being in such excellent shape.

By the end of the tournament, the areas about the baselines, where players have been digging in and serving for two weeks, are worn down to dirt plots, but they are still smooth. The different courts also vary somewhat in their speed. Most are fairly similar, but the Number One Court, which has the second largest seating capacity on the grounds, is noticeably faster than Centre Court and all the others. No one quite knows why. It has been this way for years and remains this way. Yet despite all these variations and the natural man-made tournament erosion, the courts remain true and fit.

Obviously then, the major credit goes to the men who tend the courts. These men have great pride in the work they do on the courts—an attitude that is never found in the States—and a pride that in many cases has been passed on for generations, as I learned soon after I first arrived at Wimbledon in June of 1935.

We got off the boat train from Plymouth and checked into our London hotel early in the evening, around six. Already I was excited. I had heard so much about Wimbledon for so long that I was not going to stay away for even one more day. I tried without success to talk Mako into coming out to the courts with me, so I hailed a cab and headed out to Wimbledon by myself.

It was about seven when I arrived, and there did not seem to be a person there. I peeked around, wandering through the ivied aisles that run between the outside courts, and then I turned back and headed toward the Centre Court. I looked around until at last I found an opening and moved down a passageway. It was dark, and suddenly I came to its end and burst out into the stadium arena itself. There was no net up, but I just naturally started moving toward the court area. I was not two steps onto the grass when suddenly from somewhere above, there rang out an authoritative and literal, "Halt!" I froze.

The voice had come from high above, far up in the stands, where I could make out a lone figure. It began to wend its way down the

steps toward me. Finally, across the green it strode, and I could see
that the stern voice belonged to a pleasant-faced older man in tennis shoes. He identified himself as one of the groundskeepers. "I'm
sorry," he said politely but firmly, "but no one at all is allowed on
the courts without tennis shoes on."

I swallowed. "I'm sorry," I said quickly. "I didn't know that."
And I didn't. I have seen women in high spiked heels walk across
the courts in the Forest Hills Stadium without anyone batting an eye.
"Look, my name is Don Budge," I went on. "I'm a member of the
United States team, and we just arrived in England, and I just had
to come out and see Wimbledon. I apologize. I won't go out any
further." He acknowledged my apology. So then, I just stood there,
the sun beginning to lower at last, this warm, kindly older gentleman in tennis shoes beside me, looking out at this magnificent,
lush court and the stately, dark spectator stands that surround it.
It was as impressive and as striking as I had imagined it would be.

Now quickly—fade out that scene and jump ahead a couple of
weeks. The setting is exactly the same, but now those still, bare
stands are thronged and excited. The camera zooms in on the same
wide-eyed American kid who had not even known that he could
not stride the sacred soil of Wimbledon in his hard-heeled shoes.
Only now, there I am in my tennis whites, scampering around the
court in the quarter-finals. His very first Wimbledon and the awe-
struck kid Budge is in the quarters against Bunny Austin, England's number-two player, the dapper Britisher who was the first
man in history to wear shorts at Wimbledon. I had already knocked
off Adrian Quist, who was third-seeded, and Christian Bousses,
France's top player. I was the dark horse of the field, fighting for a
chance at the semifinals of the championship of the world.

In keeping with the best of such drama, I lose the first set to Austin, 3-6. The second I come back, the set see-saws, and at last I pull
it out 10-8 to even the match. The crowd sighs. The local favorite
has lost a set, but there is a special empathy for the gangling redheaded kid. And now the momentum is mine. I win the third set
6-4 and take the lead in the fourth. Win it, and the match is mine,
and I am in the semifinals against Cramm. But then, suddenly, just

as we begin to play a point in one of the last, most crucial games, the crowd begins to rise. First one section of the stadium, then another, and finally all of Wimbledon is getting to its feet. Queen Mary has arrived.

Austin, in the court nearest to her, comes to a prompt, respectful attention. Then I, more distant on the other side of the net, notice what is happening. I turn, spot the Queen, and with an idiotic grin on my freckled face I wave gaily and call, "Hi, Queenie!" Cut—and print that. Then, quick, for good measure, splice in the scene in Oakland with Mom and Dad and Lloyd clustered about an old radio, a floppy-eared dog at their feet, while a shrill-voiced announcer shrieks, "No, I don't believe it folks, but Budge has waved to the Queen! Yessir, the kid has waved to the Queen herself! Whatdya think about that?" End of scene.

Do you think that sounds ridiculous? Incredible? Impossible? Well, more than thirty years after the alleged incident, I still find people whose first question to me is, What happened the time you waved to Queen Mary?

And the answer I give—the same one I have always given to everyone except Queen Mary herself—is that I did *not* wave to Queen Mary or anyone else and I did *not* say a word.

The fact is, as far as I can tell, that only one person in the entire stadium even imagined that I waved, and that was the British newspaperman who wrote up the incident the next day. No one even mentioned the episode to me until after it had appeared in print. Indeed, I didn't hear a great deal about it until months after it had supposedly happened, after the story spread and became embellished and picked up credence through constant retelling. But eventually it gained such a widespread notice that, in print, it came to be tacked onto my name as if it were part of it, an anchored apposition, as in, "Don Budge, the lanky redhead who waved to Queen Mary from the Centre Court of Wimbledon. . . ."

Denials did me no good, for they could never catch up with the spreading legend. Two years after the match, before I played in my first Wimbledon Final, against Cramm, we were invited to Queen Mary's box. We nodded and sat beside her. The first thing she said was, "You know, Mr. Budge, I did not see you a few years ago when you waved to me, but had I, I want you to know that I would have waved back."

That was the only time I ever failed to deny the wave, but the Queen was so gracious a lady and what she said to me was so well-intentioned that I certainly was not going to contradict her. I'm more chagrined than angry that the story still keeps popping up. The only person I have ever truly wanted to take issue with on the subject was the one man who said—and wrote—that I did wave. Conceivably he could have misinterpreted my action, but since no one else in all the 18,000 did, I remain a bit skeptical about either his eyesight or his intentions.

What actually happened lacked any special significance at all. The Queen made her arrival, and I was quite prepared for that eventuality, as all the players had been schooled in how to conduct themselves upon the entrance of the Queen. We were told to abandon playing the point the moment either one of us became aware of her presence—and that was immediately obvious since the whole stadium stood up almost *en masse* practically at the instant that she appeared. The players were then to stand at attention until she was seated and bade us go on.

In this case, Queen Mary entered right after Austin and I had completed a point, so the game was not even disrupted. I was half turned away, ready to go back to the baseline to begin the next point. Bunny, in the court nearest to the Queen's box, was facing in her direction when she appeared, so he saw her right away. I realized the Queen was there a second or two later, and turned back to acknowledge her. In doing so, I reflexively took advantage of the break to perform a gesture that I probably repeated fifty or a hundred times in every match I played. I raised my arm at about a forty-five-degree angle, so that I could wipe the sweat from my forehead on the short sleeve of my right arm. That was all. I dropped the arm quickly and never said a word. The Queen sat down, nodded to us, and I promptly went back to the baseline, unfairly and unknowingly destined to become one of the biggest American boobs ever to see royalty.

At any rate, I did beat Austin, and though I lost to Cramm the next day, my performance helped me to be chosen for the Interzone matches against the Germans. Then, after winning those, we moved on to the Challenge Round against Great Britain, and I was back on the Centre Court against Austin a month after our first match. This time I was not waving to anybody, but I was not playing very well either and I lost to Austin in four sets. This was to be the only Davis Cup meeting in which I ever lost a singles match. I also lost to Perry, and Allison lost both his matches as well. The British whitewashed us 5-0. It was the first time in twenty-four years that the United States had been shut out in Davis Cup play.

No one had really expected the British to sweep us. The bookies had made us only 7-4 underdogs, which is pretty respectable. But we did know that we had to take the singles from Austin and the doubles if we were to win, for Perry was the absolute best of the amateur world then, and the chance of either Allison or myself beating Perry was remote. For all practical purposes, then, the outcome was settled in the very opening match, when Allison, ahead two sets to one, lost the next two sets and the match to Austin.

Then I took the court against Perry. He slaughtered me. I managed to win one set from him, but the rest of the match he dominated: 6-0, 6-8, 6-3, 6-4. It was the first time I had ever played Perry for high stakes, and I was positively overwhelmed by him. He was so fast, both afoot and with his racket, that I came to feel like a street brawler, who, floored, would climb to one knee and then get knocked down again. I could never even struggle to my feet. In the vernacular, I never knew what hit me.

Perry's major weapon was his forehand. He could do so much with the shot, change direction on it so quickly and deceptively, that you had to expect to put your running shoes on whenever you hit to Fred's right. It was seldom that he made an error with the shot. He could put you in trouble, almost in one motion, by flipping his forehand on the rise, on the short hop, and then following it into the net. Certainly Fred's forehand was as important to him as my backhand was to me, and later, when we were playing each other regularly on the pro tour, our matches often came down to this basic question: Which was better, his forehand or my backhand? I would not suggest that Fred's forehand was the very greatest. Cramm, for instance, had technically as good a shot, though that was probably not so obvious since Gottfried was about a step slower than Perry. I even liked Ellie Vines's forehand better than Perry's because I believe that the eastern grip that Ellie used was better suited to the shot than the Continental grip that Perry used. However, what made Perry's forehand so outstanding was not just the shot itself—though it was marvelous enough if you wanted to examine it under a microscope—but the manner in which he could use it to influence and better his whole game. His net play, for instance, was exemplified less by the final stabbing volley than by the fact that he could reach the net so easily behind a forehand to make the volley.

Naturally, when you played Fred, you concentrated on keeping the ball away from his forehand, but you had to keep him honest and hit an occasional shot to that side. If you didn't, he would be so able to anticipate a backhand that he would play more to that side—cheat over a few steps. If he could get away with that, then he could start hitting winners from that side, which he normally would never even try to do. Fred's backhand was invariably a very defensive shot. In comparing our weaker shots, I think my forehand was better than his backhand.

One of the more unusual compliments I've received, and one that I always savored, came from Tilden after he had played me for the first time at Wembley, shortly after I turned pro. "You know, Don," he said, "I kept hearing about your backhand for all these years, but you only missed your forehand five times in two sets. You may be more dangerous with your backhand, but I really believe your forehand is steadier."

In my-backhand-v.-his-forehand battles with Fred I had one advantage. Players are so used to working on an opponent's backhand, since it is almost invariably the weaker shot, that when they played me, even though they were consciously trying to keep the ball away from my backhand, their instincts would often overcome even the most meticulous planning, and they would suddenly hit to my left without even realizing it. Attacking to the backhand is so ingrained with most players that even when Fred was playing me night after night on tour, he would sometimes forget and hit to my backhand.

Often when this happened I would retaliate by returning intentionally to Fred's forehand. He would begin the sequence by forgetting my strength and pushing a shot cross-court to my backhand. Then, instead of hitting back cross-court to his backhand, I would surprise him and flip my backhand down the line. The shot was directed to his forehand, but Fred would have a good run across the court for it, and he would have to scramble to reach it. Usually, he would get the shot back, but then he was well out of position and I had virtually the whole court to make my return in. I could, for instance, now hit cross-court and make him try to run back and make a more difficult backhand in return.

I think that too many players concentrate on the forehand at the expense of the backhand, so that the backhand becomes a defensive shield and of no value to the attack. But however strong your backhand, you absolutely must have a solid forehand. I found that out when I first played on grass and discovered that my western grip was deficient. My game was certainly more effective after I changed the grip.

Briefly, the western grip may be achieved by laying your racket on a flat surface, then picking it up with a handshake hold. This should bring your hand one eighth of a turn further around to the outside of the handle than on the eastern grip. The eastern grip, remember, is obtained by shaking hands with the racket held in a position perpendicular to the ground, so that it would rest on its frame if put down. The Continental grip is essentially the same as the backhand grip, a one eighth turn to the *in*side from the eastern grip.

A good forehand shot is best produced by getting your racket back early. Then, when you move it forward, hit up slightly, pointing your racket in the direction you want the ball to go on your follow-through. This is technically advisable because it is founded in logic. After all, most players do hit the forehand the hardest of their ground strokes, so there is less arc and less margin for error. A hard forehand hit with no lift to the swing is simply going to be moving with too much velocity to fall within the court. A lift in the swing provides topspin.

The only accommodation to the rule of level swing must come on a high bounce, when the ball reaches you above your shoulder level. Then you must hold the racket so that its head is above the wrist. This time, the best you can manage is a level swing, straight through, or downward, in something of a chop if the ball has bounced extremely high. But, after all, such a bounce is difficult and unusual, and seldom can it be turned into a winner. It is best to return it with satisfactory pace and direction, keep the ball in play, and look for the big shot later in the exchange.

On all other forehand shots, however, you must strive for a swing that has the wrist firm, with the racket almost parallel to the ground at the point of contact. The reason I switched to the eastern grip was that I found I could not hit the low-bouncing grass-court shots with the western grip. To hit a low forehand, you must drop the racket head below the level of where you will contact the ball, and hit up as well as forward, letting the racket head do the work. Bend your knees and get the whole body down to the ball. It is a great deal easier to lower the racket (and then swing up) than to lower your body, but to hit low-bouncing balls, you must do both to obtain consistent results. You've seen what happens when you don't—the ball flies out of the court like a rocket.

In approaching a forehand shot, the right-hander should pivot on his right foot from the anticipatory position of facing the net. You move the left foot forward so that as the ball comes, you are sideways to the net. The movement should throw most of your weight back on your right foot, and, just as naturally, let your free left arm swing out forward toward the net, as an effective counterbalance.

The ball is nearing you. Now swing your racket arm back in an opposing arc from the left arm. Do not twist the racket. There is no value in doing so, and it is only going to require more effort to untwist it when you bring the racket forward to make contact. The forehand is a simple shot, and the less wasted motion the better.

At the peak of the backswing the racket should thus be open-faced slightly and ready to move forward on the ball.

At this point in the swing, the racket head drops slightly below the wrist. Now, as you begin to swing into the ball, as your weight thrusts forward onto the left foot, you will hit up onto the ball. This will provide it with the natural topspin you need to keep the ball in the court.

Contact is best made in front of you—about eighteen inches forward of your left hip. Your racket arm is extended, not only so that you can meet the ball at the top of its bounce but also so that you can hit it at a comfortable distance from your body. Both leverage and control are quickly lost if the ball is hit too close to you.

The hit made, now you complete your swing, raising the racket in a final slight upswing that is both natural and confident. And once again, remember: Stop the follow-through so that the racket is pointing in the direction you want the ball to go.

It is impossible to dictate a formula that defines exactly where the weight and feet should lie for proper shot placement. There is no trick. The ball you want to direct cross-court is naturally going to be hit slightly more in front of your body than is a shot intended for down the line. Perfect the solid, stationary, standard old unromantic hit. Then, when your body finds the nuances of direction and weight-shift through practice, the stroke itself will not be disturbed.

Perry's magic forehand was on a level far above mere mechanical excellence. The sheer superiority of Perry's forehand was the foundation upon which he built his complete winning game. It was also a sleight of forehand, though, and it was not until two years after he beat me so soundly in the Challenge Round of '35 that I was fully able to divine the secret that made his forehand so devastating.

4

Learning by Losing

The period following my loss to Perry in the '35 Challenge Round became something of a regrouping. My game did not decline. You could not even say that it remained static. But there were none of the highlights of that first burst of glory, so that it at least appeared to be in eclipse until my meeting with Fred in the finals of the '36 Forest Hills set my career in motion again.

In safe retrospect perhaps it is possible to assume that the interim period was necessary. I had come fast and far, but for the moment about as far as I could go. At the end of '35 I shot up to number two in the national rankings, behind only Allison, who won at Forest Hills. I lost to Bitsy Grant in the quarters that year, in a match that was interrupted by rain and a weird, eerie twilight that made Queens feel like Armageddon. Bitsy was only five feet five, a great little retriever, who by the time he was through had beaten just about everyone at least once. Still, I passed him in the rankings for the first time. This was also the first time I was ranked ahead of Parker.

As I had done the year before, I passed up tournament play over the winter and went home to practice and exercise with Tom Stow. I felt that I was in good shape for my first big match of the year—against Jack Crawford in the second match of the first day's play of the Interzone Davis Cup Finals. The match was held at the Germantown Cricket Club in Philadelphia on May 30.

Summer suddenly arrived with the whoosh of a flash fire, and by the time Crawford and I took the court, the temperature in the sun was well over one hundred. The humidity was as high and debilitating as it usually is when extreme temperatures come to the eastern seaboard. I can remember having leg cramps of a serious nature only twice in my career. This was one of those times.

Crawford was number two in the world after Perry then, but he was also several years older than I, and, to boot, he was asthmatic. The weather, as enervating as it was, should have existed to my advantage—or, at any rate, less to my disadvantage than to Crawford's. I began beautifully too, winning the first two sets with the loss of only five games, and should have been in a position to annihilate the world's number-two player in straight sets. This prospect, however, occasioned me to think too much. I became too cautious in the face of such an eminently agreeable prospect, and I started to play safely. My greatest error was my failure to continue to charge the net. I let the match lapse into more of a baseline game, and Crawford, who possessed a marvelous forehand, was given the chance to crank it up and force me onto the defensive.

He turned the match around completely. In fact, he took the next two sets with as much dispatch—losing only five games—as I had the first two. Moreover, Jack kept his momentum and rushed to a 5-3 lead in the fifth set. I did win that game, but he came back again and had me but two points from defeat, 5-4 and 30-all, in the next game. I survived that scare too, to tie the match once more.

I was revived, and confident for the first time in a long while, but I was unable to break through Crawford's superb defensive game. In the awful heat of the afternoon, defense was, too, a more stationary game, and if it came to a matter of attrition Jack may have had the edge. As it developed, neither one of us could have played one more shot than we had to. I finally got a set point on him at 12-11, and hit a back-court crossing shot to his backhand. Crawford reached for it and went for broke with a crisp backhand of his own down the line. I chased after it and began to reach out desperately for it, but the shot passed me hardly as I began to swing. Luckily, it fell out only by inches.

In reaching, though, I had extended myself that bit too much. I had cramps in my thighs, and I could hardly move. Walter Pate finally reached me and helped me to my feet. I turned, under his support, to go to the net and shake hands with Crawford, but just as I did I saw Jack waver, swoon, and at last fall flat out in a dead faint. In this match, both the winner and loser had to be literally carried off the court.

My own case was so bad, however, that the cramps kept returning. I was first laid out between chairs by the side of the court, and when the pain subsided sufficiently, Captain Pate piled Gene Mako and myself into the Buick convertible he had, so we could get right over to the Merion Cricket Club, where our team was staying, and rest up for our doubles match the next day. Pate had Gene and me sit in the rumble seat, and suddenly, after he had driven us for a while, my cramp returned. I honestly doubt whether I was ever in more excruciating pain.

I screamed, but that was of no use, so hardly recognizing what I was doing I began to straighten my leg out in that tight little space. I stretched my legs so hard, so reflexively, that I actually put a bend in the panel that divided the rumble seat from the rest of the car. It was a metal panel, about the thickness of a fender, I suppose. I pushed it in so hard that we had to stop on the way home at an auto-repair shop to get the piece banged back into shape.

I was bothered no further in the matches with the Australians, and rather forgot about the matter. I should have considered the implications more seriously, however. After all, I was still two weeks short of my twenty-first birthday; Crawford was much older and asthmatic. Yet I had not been able to dominate the match as it progressed. The five sets took almost three hours, which is a good day's work but not an exceptional amount of time. I should have been in better shape at the end, but in victory I failed to appreciate the omens, and I would not understand them, it turned out, until the end of the long summer.

I also won my other singles match against the Aussies, beating Quist after his team had already clinched the Interzone victory at 3-1. Adrian had beaten Wilmer Allison on the opening day, and Crawford took the deciding point by also beating Allison, but we really lost the tie the day before in the doubles, when Mako and I were teamed together for our first important Davis Cup play. We were up against Quist and Crawford, and how Gene and I ever managed to lose is still an irritating subject for me. We took the first two sets with ease from the Aussies, then turned right around and lost the next two, the same way I had let Crawford catch up in our singles match. But this time, in the doubles, Gene and I righted ourselves and had the Aussies 3-0 and 4-1 in the last set. At that point we proceeded not only to lose the next five games, but also to score only six points in the progress. It was a dismal cave-in, and beating Quist the next day after the matter was settled was of little consolation.

I beat Quist again in straight sets a few weeks later in the quarter-finals at Wimbledon, but all that accomplished was to provide me with the dubious privilege of playing Perry in the semis, and I found out quickly enough that I was no match for him yet. I won the first set 7-5 by taking four straight games from 3-5 when Fred's forehand suddenly found one of its rare feeble moments in history, but he settled down in the next set and rushed me off the court 6-4, 6-3, 6-4. As before against Perry, I remained under his domination. He was always on top of me, rattling shots back as quickly as I could right myself from the one before.

Then Fred went on to take his third consecutive Wimbledon title when Gottfried pulled his hamstring in the finals. Perry was now the absolute master of the amateurs. No man since has won three straight Wimbledons, and the others who managed that feat before Fred, played in the days when Wimbledon still had a Challenge Round and the defending champion, as in the Davis Cup, had only to play once for the title.

Perry had also won twice previously at Forest Hills, in 1933 and 1934. He had lost the following year in the semis to Allison after he took a bad fall early in the match. A victory in '36 would thus give him three United States titles to match his three Wimbledons. Perry had also brought Great Britain the Davis Cup for four years running. There were no more amateur worlds for him to conquer, and the pros were increasing their offers. Ellie Vines was dominating the professionals in the same manner that Fred was lording it over the amateurs. Theirs was an obvious rivalry, and one that would be even more attractive if Perry could cap his amateur career by winning his third United States Nationals title.

He did get that victory, of course, and in fact, Fred remains the last man to win the United States championship three times. I should have had that '36 title, though I have no excuse and the only one I can blame for my loss in the finals to Fred is myself.

That year during the tournament Gene Mako and I stayed with Walter Pate and Mrs. Pate at their home in Glen Cove, Long Island. For wild excitement at night we would usually play a few hands of cards. Then, no later than about ten-thirty or eleven, Gene and I would go down to the nearest drugstore and order a couple of those extra-thick milkshakes, the ones you have to eat with a spoon. Usually, I went for chocolate. Then we'd go right off to bed. It certainly seemed like a harmless enough nightcap.

About midway through the tournament, though, I was practicing one day on a sidecourt with Ellie Vines. Suddenly I was weak-kneed and woozy. I could feel my stomach searching for help. "Hold it, Ellie," was about all I could say, and then I absolutely tore to the locker room. I was perfectly grass-green by the time I got there, which was just in time. The chocolate, the milk, the rich ice cream, and all the other sweets that I had refused to deny myself had turned my stomach sour in the September heat. It is not the kind of glamorous disability that athletes would prefer if they have to have one, but there I was—wounded with an upset stomach.

My stamina was gone. In the fourth round I met Gene Smith, who was a good California player but one I should have had no trouble with. Smith took a set off me, and our match was fairly close throughout. I defeated John McDiarmid in the quarters much more easily, but then I came up against Parker in the semifinals. Luckily, I beat Frankie in straight sets, and then I straightaway collapsed. Had Parker been able to extend me just a bit further, I'm sure that he would have taken me in five.

I came up against Perry, then, with conflicting emotions. Since that exhibition at Eastbourne earlier in the summer, when I had beaten him when he was out there playing for the exercise, I genuinely believed that he was not invincible. On the other hand, I recognized that I was more vulnerable than usual, since my stomach miseries had not improved at all.

The day for the finals came up ghastly, dark, and drizzly, but still the West Side Tennis Club was all but packed. Had it not been for the rain it surely would have been an overflow. The fans, like myself, knew that this was my last chance in a major international tournament to beat Perry.

Fred and I and the rain split the first two sets three ways. I won the opener 6-2, and he won the second set by the same score, but before he did, the downpour came and halted play for half an hour. I returned to the locker room to fret. I always hated interruptions of this sort. I could never really learn to relax and take the pause in stride. I tended to become edgy and more uncomfortable. As a matter of fact, I even disliked the ten-minute break that, except at Wimbledon, is always accorded after the third set in a five-set match. At the British championships they just play a match straight through, and I prefer that system.

In this match, it seemed that we could never get started. After the first rain break we came back, he won the set, and then we moved into the third, which I won 8-6. Now at this point we were required to take the regular rest period, and then hardly had we gotten underway in the fourth set than the rains came again, and we had to quit one more time for another ten minutes or so.

This meant we had had a total of almost an hour's rest since the match began, and yet I still found myself falling into exhaustion. I was no match at all for Fred in the fourth set, where he won 6-1, so I kept my running to a bare minimum once he moved well ahead, and tried to conserve what energy I had left for the final set.

We held serve to 3-2, my favor, and then I got the break for 4-2. Promptly, I permitted Fred to break me back. My serve was a dishrag. However, tired as I was, I was able to break him back again, so I stood at 5-3, serving for the national championship of my country against the number-one player in the world. All I had to do was hold my serve one more time.

I could not. I was so exhausted in reaching up to hit my serve that I felt as if I were leaning on the ball. There was no life in my shots. The stretching and reaching for the serve particularly wore on me. He broke me again—our fourth loss of service in a row—held his own serve at last, and tied the set at 5-all.

I was to get other chances, though. In fact, in the sixteenth game, when I was ahead 8-7, I came within two points of victory, but I could never come any closer. Once I did hold, it took me most of his service game to recuperate, so that I could begin the process over again.

It is ironic that Fred had a cramp in his leg and was probably operating with as much discomfort and disability as I was. This balancing factor is why I particularly emphasize that I have no right to excuses whatsoever. If I had known about Fred's cramp, though, I surely would have tried to exploit it. I would have hit one shot wide to his forehand and made him chase the ball. He might have retrieved the ball, but could he have gotten back? And if so, could he have managed the chore repeatedly? But I was not aware of his disability, and without the knowledge, I was not about to play to Perry's forehand. The chance was gone before I knew it existed. In the twenty-third game he at last broke through me again and wrapped up the title 13-11 by holding his serve in the next game.

I never lost a championship so narrowly. It is a frustrating experience under any circumstances, but that I was sure I lost because of my own negligence in not properly conditioning myself made the defeat even more irritating for me. When I returned to Oakland a few weeks later, my primary concern was not with strengthening my game, but with strengthening myself. For both self-improvement and technical advancement, this was to be the most important winter of my career. I was a stronger man with a new game when the off-season ended.

I realize that every athlete must find his own best methods and schedule, but I still feel that too many of today's players do not give themselves a full, necessary respite from the game. They grow stale. Tennis these days is increasingly a year-round game, and the opportunity is there to play a full twelve months a year in gracious surroundings and against good competition. But to take unbridled advantage of these obvious possibilities seems to me to consider only the short-term dividends. The evidence is overwhelming in all sports that a full year's schedule destroys the chance for peak timing. Baseball players who attempt to play a season of winter ball invariably peter out by August. Golfers take off from competition for whole weeks at a time, no matter how lucrative are the tournaments that they must pass up. Even Thoroughbred horses must periodically be excused from competition before they lose their edge and interest.

Besides, it is my feeling that a rest from the sport not only eventually profits one's athletic development and proficiency but is also a mental refresher. It is a good idea for all players, regardless of level of competition, to keep that point in mind and to take a vacation from the game occasionally, just as you do from work.

It was my own program to abandon tennis for six weeks each year, beginning early in October. I found plenty of other good exercise, but I mean that I literally would not touch a racket for six weeks.

Actually, the first two weeks of my exile were a pleasure to endure. I was delighted to be away from the courts. Then I would begin to get itchy and start dropping over to the Berkeley Tennis Club to see my friends. After just a few quick glances at some rallies I would be ready to go back on the court. Somehow I managed to stay away, though, so when I finally did come back after a month and a half, the tedious practice was fun and exhilarating.

The winter of 1936-1937, however, I really started to work the day I got home, because I was determined to build myself up, to develop fifth-set stamina, and particularly to strengthen my stomach muscles. It was they that had failed so disastrously against Perry, especially at the serve, which demands a stretching and reaching that requires hard, taut muscles. A soft stomach goeth before a fault.

I immediately cut out of my diet all the foods that had turned my stomach sour: chocolates, pastries and other sweets, and fried foods as well. As soon as I got back, long before I began practicing on the courts, I undertook a program of special physical exercises. These exercises were nothing new and original even then, but they have always been, and still are, among the most effective exercises for strengthening the abdominal muscles.

In the first of the two basic exercises I would lie on the ground on my back, hands clasped behind my head. Then I would raise my trunk until I could touch my knees with my elbows—hands still clasped at the nape of the neck. I would repeat this exercise twenty or thirty times a day, increasing the number of times as I became more fit and able.

Second, I also performed a similar number of deep knee bends. Standing erect, feet spread a few inches apart, hands on hips, you squat down and stand up, over and over. It's a pretty unromantic and familiar exercise, as anybody who has ever served a day in the armed forces knows, but it is valuable and reliable work.

Running, of course, is good at any age for any game, including just living. I took to running many miles a day. I had a shiny new Packard 120 that I had bought with my savings from working as a part-time shipping clerk, and I would drive up into the Berkeley Hills and park the Packard in the foothills, out along Tunnel Road.

One difficulty with keeping up your running is the matter of incentive. Jogging along, day in, day out, can grow boring. To contend somewhat with that problem, I had the view. From where I was running, along the crest of the Berkeleys, I could look down, over Oakland and Berkeley, down onto the Bay and Frisco. (You are not supposed to call it "Frisco," I know. The natives get very agitated about that, but I always do—not to be difficult, but to be endearing. I've always had great affection for San Francisco. It's a magnificent city. When I say "Frisco," I say it because that is the way it has always been to me, and it's too late to stop.)

Anyway, it was a beautiful view, and on the days when the weather was truly clear, you could see past the Bay, past Alcatraz, past Frisco, right out to the Golden Gate, to Sausalito beyond, and even, sometimes, to the Pacific. It made running a great deal more satisfying, and after I parked the car I would *walk* up the hills, and then run across them (where the view was) and down, and then walk back to the car. Pretty soon I was able to run all the way up and down and back to the car.

Running improves wind, of course, but perhaps even more important to me, it also flattens and tightens the stomach muscles. I did not always have the Berkeley Hills at my disposal, but wherever I traveled, I made an effort to run as much as possible. Also, for the rest of my amateur career and even a year or so into my first pro season—a period, say, of about three years altogether—I do not believe that I missed doing my exercises more than a total of six or seven days all told.

Aside from the simple matter of staying on your feet and keeping up throughout a match, the service is most demanding of top shape. And make no mistake: The serve is, unequivocally, the most important shot in tennis. Since the shot is all yours too, it should be the easiest one to master. My serve was never my major weapon—as, for instance, it was for Vines and is for Gonzales—but my serve was consistent. Once I strengthened my muscles to the point where I could physically manage to maintain a steady serve, it never let me down. I do not mean it always won for me. It didn't. But it never abandoned me. With a steady serve you can at least stay in the game.

If the backhand is like hitting a baseball, a serve is like throwing one, which is why it was so natural for Alice Marble to rifle those pegs in from the San Francisco Seals' outfield. The girl who can serve will not, as the expression goes, "throw like a girl," for the motions are closely related. In serving, your elbow should be kept high and away from the body, just as if you were trying to throw for distance. Arthur Ashe usually has a magnificent serve, but he also has whole matches in which his serve is spotty. The reason for this unfortunate inconsistency is that Ashe tucks his elbow in too close to his body. Anyone can hit a good serve sometimes, despite keeping the elbow in too tight, but the margin of error is reduced to a minimum when the elbow is up and away. Arthur is on or off; there is no in-between for him.

His serve came back just in time for him to win the biggest match of his life, when he beat Tom Okker of the Netherlands in five sets to win the first United States Open. Before the match I went over to a sidecourt at Forest Hills to watch Arthur warm up. He saw me and shook his head. "I'm having trouble with my serve again," he said.

There is just no reason why Arthur should have this problem. I simply cannot understand why Pancho Gonzales, who works with Arthur and is close to him, does not try to convince Ashe to keep his elbow high and away, as he does himself.

Pancho never had any bad serving days. Sometimes he was a little better than others, but he was never off. Watching the best servers, such as Gonzales, or Vines, or Kramer, always made me think of a great snake uncoiling. There should be nothing jerky at all to the motion—only a natural, rhythmic unwinding. Sammy Snead provides the same sensation for me when he hits a golf ball. As good as he is and as lithe as he is, there is no reason whatsoever why Ashe should not look as smooth serving a tennis ball.

The serve originated in tennis as an expediency, the necessary evil for getting the ball in play. It has evolved into the very heart of the attack, and, in fact, it even sets the tone of the action that determines the outcome of almost every point. Besides being the salient of strategy, it is also a great psychological factor. Usually my whole game picked up when I was serving well, but if I was serving poorly, I had to guard against worrying about a bad serve I had already hit instead of concentrating on the volley I had yet to play.

To hit a serve in singles, position yourself just to the side of mid-court. If you move too far over, you leave too much of the court wide open for your opponent to return down the line. You should stand just a couple of inches behind the baseline to lessen the possibility of jumping your forward foot over the line and foot-faulting. The forward left foot (for a right-hander) should be about eighteen inches in front of the back right foot, the same way, approximately, that a pitcher stands on the mound. Let your body relax as you prepare to begin the stroke. To steady the racket, cradle the racket throat in the fingers of the left hand. The racket should be gripped firmly with the right hand, but not in a death squeeze. Similarly, the ball(s) should be held in the fingers, not in the palm of your left hand. On the first serve, if it is more comfortable for you, place the extra ball in your pocket, although I advise against this because of the delay in fishing it out. The primary idea at this stage is to get comfortable. Not until you are should you shift your balance to your back foot and prepare for the toss and the swing.

The stroke itself begins for both arms simultaneously. The importance of the action of the left arm is not to be minimized either, for if the ball is not tossed properly, the most beautiful stroke in the world will not be sufficient to erase the error already made. In the serve, your right arm better know what your left arm is doing.

The toss occurs at the same time as you begin your racket backswing. The ball should be thrown lazily, high and forward. How high you throw the ball is determined by how high you can reach. You want to make contact with the ball at the apex of your swing, so the perfect throw is one that sends the ball a couple of inches higher than your racket can reach. You will hit the ball, then, just as it has begun its fall. Some coaches maintain that you should make contact at the top of the ball's rise, but I do not advocate this. It is best to adjust your toss to a continuous swing of the racket, rather than adjust your racket swing to a faulty toss. For example, if your toss is too high, you must adjust your swing by pausing somewhere, thus breaking the rhythm and momentum and sacrificing power. If your serve is too low, you must hurry through the swing to avoid hitting the ball on the handle, thus sacrificing control. The ideal toss will bring ball and racket together at the top of your swing as your smooth, unbroken motion increases in speed from the start of the swing to the moment of impact.

In any event, do not make the mistake of trying to hit down on the ball. The ball already has its own downward motion, and needs no extra direction from you. Instead of hitting down, hit straight away from you, as if you were actually trying to throw the racket into the service area across the net.

Now for the swing itself.

Remember, it begins as a simultaneous countermotion to the toss. Bring the racket down and around in an easy arc, keeping the wrist in a loose uncocked position. As the racket reaches the nadir of its arc, begin to shift your weight forward upon the left foot. It is also at approximately this moment that the ball begins its soft release from your fingers.

Your pendulum swing continues. Do not cock the wrist in preparation for the hit until the racket is well overhead (and still somewhat behind you). Then, when your elbow has reached the height of your shoulder—though far wide of it—break your wrist. The racket head drops and the forward thrust begins.

You are stretched to a full reach now on your toes. Your stomach muscles are pulled tight. Indeed, as the wrist snaps the racket forward and you swing to hit the ball, which should be about two feet in front of the baseline, you should actually feel as if you are trying to throw the racket. I continue to repeat that analogy because it is an entirely accurate one. If you throw-serve properly, your rear foot (the right one) should come forward naturally as you finish the stroke, so that you are moving toward the net, ready for the return.

Contrary to the more romantic illusion of the bullet serve conquering all, speed of the serve is not nearly so vital as the control. This so-called flat or cannonball serve is hit with less spin than the safer second serve. "Flat serve" is a misnomer, since the serve must be hit with a certain amount of spin in order to control it. The flat serve and the slice are both hit with swings that draw the racket across the body, ending up on your left side. These are the more common serves, for the American twist seems to have become almost obsolete. The twist is, I think, the safest of all second serves to hit, producing, as it does, a difficult high bounce to the backhand. Cramm hit perhaps the greatest of the American twists. It is a hard shot to make because the ball must be thrown nearly behind you, forcing you to arch your back to reach the ball, hitting up into the ball rather than straight out as in the normal first serve, with the swing finishing on the right side of the body, rather than across it on the left.

The first serve (or, really, the "big" serve, as it is most often referred to) is the more difficult serve to control. In fact, if you hit the serve too flat, I don't believe you can control it sufficiently to make the extra power worthwhile. It can become a runaway truck. For the slice serve, bevel the racket and toss the ball farther away from you, to the right side.

The glamour drawn to the powerful big serve has definitely

caused a decline in interest in the second serve. I don't want to fall into that old-timers' trap of muttering something that sounds suspiciously like "they don't do things the way they used to," but in this instance it is difficult to avoid the cliché. Not enough attention is paid to the second serve. I think (and both Kramer and Gonzales agree with me) that, in the long run, it is more profitable to have a good second serve than a spectacular first one.

Kramer had the best second service of all. With speed reduced and less of a factor, the second serve puts its emphasis on placement, and Kramer had the foremost ability consistently to spot the ball. He could repeatedly serve within a two-foot-square block—that distant little territory to the rear and side of the service area. Vines, Cramm, and Lester Stoefen were other exponents of a fine second serve, and Gonzales, for all the talk about his big cannonball, also has always exhibited a good second serve and an understanding of how important the shot is. Tilden, on the other hand, always failed to impress me with his second serve. Henner Henkel, too, served a cream puff for dessert, not at all in the same class as his powerful, beefsteak first serve.

As a rule, modern players do not practice the second serve enough. The most obvious exception would be Rod Laver, whose second serve is always reliable and often even a most formidable weapon. Part of the reason for this is that Laver is a left-hander, and a southpaw serve always bounces differently from the right-handed serve you have come to expect. The left-handed serve may not be truly more effective, but it never fails to surprise.

Indeed, Laver reminds me quite a bit of John Doeg, who won the U.S. Nationals title in 1930 over Tilden. John never achieved the greatest stature in the sport because many facets of his game, his ground strokes, for instance, were somewhat lacking. But John Doeg was one of the most effective servers of all time.

The argument about who is the premier server is invariably restricted to include only Tilden, Vines, and Gonzales, but you should have *seen* Doeg. He did not hit it quite as hard as Vines, but with that big left-handed move, he came around with a slice that actually knocked the ball lopsided. I mean that. Doeg turned the ball into an ellipse, and try hitting that back. The players referred to it as "John's egg-ball." Besides, when Doeg's serve in the ad court bounced it would fly crazily off to the side, and no man could chase it down. If you did manage to get the ball back, just reaching the return carried you so far out of the court that there was no chance that you could make it back in time to get Doeg's return. However, since John had little more proclivity for returning serve than losing serve, all his matches were forever running to 18-16. You never broke Doeg's serve. You outlasted it.

But if John had a devastating serve, there is no doubt in my mind that Ellie Vines had the fastest. His serve velocity was measured once at 121 m.p.h. Lester Stoefen's was clocked at 120 m.p.h., and Pancho's at 118 m.p.h. Figures aside, however, I would still say that no one has ever hit a faster ball than Ellie. I stood in awe of his power. Every stroke he hit exploded. In fact, when Fred Perry turned pro to tour against Vines, I was so impressed by Ellie's power that I felt sure that he would annihilate Fred.

If I had to single out two matches that were most influential to my game and philosophy—and, in fact, career—both matches would involve Perry. The first was our finals match at Forest Hills in '36, when I was forced to realize the need for better conditioning. The second significant match of Perry's came that winter, in January of 1937, only this time I was not playing Fred, but was in the umpire's chair. I was so curiously located because when the Vines-Perry tour moved into the old Chicago Arena, I was brought East on the Super Chief as a gimmick—to umpire the proceedings. In this, for me, unique capacity I had to strive for an aloof objectivity, but, as I have said, I was sure that Vines would destroy Perry.

Perry, after all, had a game that was hardly more than on a par with my own. He had defeated me in all our important meetings, but he was not so much better that I had not been able to catch him on several other occasions during his last year as an amateur. I simply could not conceive how Perry could contend with Ellie's power. As it turned out, Vines did win the tour, but hardly by the lopsided margin I envisioned.

That Fred was keeping up with Ellie was obvious from the first few games at the Arena. Sitting up there in the umpire's high chair, I had a hard time keeping score, for I was amazed from the start at the way the match was going. I had come expecting to see Vines's hard shots sending Perry scurrying all over the court. Instead, Perry was forcing Vines to run every bit as much. It made no sense to me. How could Vines, who was hitting a much heavier ball, fail to control the play?

It took some time before I caught on. Then I saw it. Perry was taking the ball on the rise, hardly six or eight inches after it had bounced—"on the short hop," as they call it in baseball. Vines, on the other hand, was waiting in a leisurely fashion and letting the ball take a nice, comfortable high bounce. By the time Ellie had wound up and hit most of his shots, the ball would often even be dropping, about to begin a second bounce. Vines was hitting the ball harder than Perry, but he took longer to do so and then he had to hit the ball a greater distance.

For his part, Perry was hitting the ball early enough to compensate for his lesser power. We are only dealing here in split seconds, but in a game so fast, instants do count. Sitting up there in the umpire's stand, directly at mid-court, my head swinging back and forth, the effect was suddenly clear and obvious. I could see the split seconds: Perry scooping up the ball, Vines rocking back for it. Before the match was even over a new concept had begun to form in my mind: Suppose a man could hit the ball as hard as Vines and take it as early as Perry? Who could beat that man?

I went back to California determined to see if I could implement that idea and turn it into a reality. It was not only a sound tennis proposition, but it also conveniently fit in with the spirit that Tom Stow was trying to instill in me. With Perry a pro, we had already set the highest hopes for '37. I was to think of myself as number one at all times. If I concentrated on that belief, we felt that I would be more likely to *play* like number one.

Joe Louis was the heavyweight champion then, and not only was he beating everyone he met, but most opponents were already intimidated by the very idea of meeting Louis even before they stepped into the ring with him. Our psychology, then, was to try and scare the opposition. I was to keep up the pressure at all times, never let up, so that playing me would be a generally unnerving and unpleasant experience. Winning, we felt, would then be made much easier for me.

Hitting the ball harder and earlier aligned with this thinking perfectly, and so in the months after the Vines-Perry match I worked almost exclusively toward these two goals. My game was not pretty at first, but then I did not concern myself too much with accuracy. It was long before I was even able to get the ball into the court with regularity. I was knocking down about every fence in the area. This is in direct contradiction to my first rule of keeping the ball in play, but I was performing a major adjustment on my game, and Stow and I felt that the priority in this exceptional case must be with perfecting the stroke. Control and nuance came later, but by the end of the training period I was able to achieve accuracy.

Largely because of this additional development, 1937 turned out to be a year that exceeded all of our expectations. I was undefeated on grass and I did not lose a singles match on any surface until September 16 in a small tournament in Chicago, where Henner Henkel beat me. By then, I had won at Wimbledon and Forest Hills and had helped return the Davis Cup to the United States for the first time in eleven years. I was voted Athlete of the Year by the American Sportswriters, and I became the first and only tennis player ever to win the Sullivan Award, which is annually presented to the world's most outstanding amateur athlete. The special glory of being the first man to win the Grand Slam has made 1938 a more memorable year, but it is difficult for me to say that '37 was any less satisfying.

My first significant competition in '37 came in the Davis Cup play against Japan. I won both my singles and joined with Mako to take the doubles as well. I repeated this performance against Australia and also, of course, against Germany (and Cramm) in those famous Interzone Finals at Wimbledon. Then we wrapped up the Challenge Round against England, 4-1.

Perry had turned pro before now, and his replacement, Charles

Hare, just could not be ranked in the same league with Fred. Our victory, then, was no surprise. Walter Pate substituted Parker in the singles for Bitsy, as he had suffered Centre Court jitters against the Germans, and Frankie split his matches. Mako and I won the doubles again, and I also beat Austin and Hare. I finished the year with a Davis Cup record of 12-0, with eight singles and four doubles victories. I think I was as proud of that as winning the major individual titles. The pros wanted to sign me up and challenge Vines, and if it had just been an individual thing, maybe I would have. I was sincere, however, in believing that if I had helped bring the Davis Cup home, I should at least try to keep it home for a year before I left the project with others. I had the idea of the Grand Slam forming in my mind in '37, but the main reason I didn't turn pro at the end of the season was because of the Davis Cup.

In the midst of our commitments for winning the cup back, I gained my first Wimbledon victory. It should have been the apex of my career, and at the time, it surely was. I do not mean to belittle it to say, however, that it happened in a way that made it a rather routine accomplishment. I was, above all, at the top of my game. At Queens, the tournament that is traditionally a good prep for Wimbledon—it is on grass and it is nearby, so you can get settled in London—I won the singles easily. Those great partners of mine, Gene Mako and Alice Marble, were in top shape too, and I won the doubles and mixed with them. So I was in good condition and in fine spirits. This is what Tom Stow and I had aimed for. Indeed, I moved into the finals without drama or difficulty, and the only trouble I then had against Cramm was of my own making. I permitted myself to be overwhelmed by the significance of the occasion.

Gottfried and I went out on the court and took that four-minute warm-up. I served and he broke me. I had lost the first set in the semis to Parker, the only set in the tournament that I had dropped, and in my mind I could visualize myself going down again already. Gottfried's high-kicker was going in consistently, and he held until 3-1 when I finally woke up and broke him back. "Budge was

78 DON BUDGE: A TENNIS MEMOIR

beginning to take the ball earlier," the London *Times* noted the next day about this part of the match. And I was, at last. My whole game took on new life and I started to force the play.

The trepidation gone, I was suddenly eager and keen, and I broke Gottfried again to lead 5-3. Then I began to shudder again. All I could keep thinking was: You're ahead, Don. You're ahead in the first set of the finals of the championship of the world. (Really, I was thinking this exactly.) Just hold your serve, Budge, and you win the first set. Just hold your serve. My whole body was shaking by the time I picked up the ball to serve, but somehow I managed to win the game at thirty and go ahead with the first set.

The momentum from that win carried me into the second set, for I broke through Cramm's serve again in the first game, and held my own for 2-0 and 3-1. Then I started that same thinking again: Budge, just remember, all you have to do is hold your serve and you're two full sets ahead for the championship of the world. The thought began to blow everything else out of my mind. Gottfried broke the serve I kept imploring myself to hold—at love—and moved ahead 4-3.

It was only then that I stopped daydreaming again, and broke him back, giving him only a point, to turn the set around once more. I finished it off at 6-4.

Now I was literally shaking. Just think, Budge, one set away, etc. Over and over. I was drowning in my own sweat, but I broke Gottfried at 2-1. Hold your serve, Budge, etc. The nearness of the possibility was beginning to overwhelm me, but I kept winning and moved ahead 5-1. I had the balls in my hand to serve it out myself and finish it. So as quickly as possible I lost my serve, winning only a single point in the process. But even with that break, Gottfried was still down 5-2, and in the next game I lasted through five deuces before I finally, desperately, won my Wimbledon.

I practically had to crawl to the net to shake hands with Gottfried, my poor friend who had now reached the finals of Wimbledon three years in a row without so much as winning a set. No player as good as Cramm ever came so close so many times without winning. He was squeezed out of the honor by Perry, myself, and then the Nazis. But even this time, his third year in a row for defeat, he was as gracious as always.

I was so limp I could hardly move. The entire match had lasted little more than an hour, yet I was distressingly overcome with exhaustion. Then, slowly, the excitement began to leave me and my strength began to flow back. At match point I had been so worn down—the thought was just so thrilling—that I was hardly able to keep from collapsing. Within five minutes after the match, however, I was fresh enough to have continued for several more sets.

It was not really a debilitating physical experience. It was only that there is something about playing for the most important title in the world that staggers you. After you have done it once, you can take things in stride and glide through a match. But you have to cross that barrier of doubt and wonderment before you can relax and enjoy the real fruits of conditioning.

Gottfried and I played for the championship of the United States at Forest Hills later in the summer, and I felt none of the trauma that I found at Wimbledon, even though the match went five sets. But it was a strange mixture of sets. I would win easily (6-1), lose with agony (7-9), win easily (6-1), and lose with agony again (3-6). I was quite sure that I was in no trouble and would win the deciding set, which, in fact, I did, 6-1. It took five sets, but all of the winning sets were 6-1 and it really seemed a great deal easier afternoon than Wimbledon had.

Perhaps the crowd helped. The Stadium was packed with 14,000 and at least 5000 had been turned away. They were all for me. I could do no wrong. It had been that way ever since the Davis Cup team and the Cup itself had returned to New York on the old SS *Washington*. They had taken our whole team and put us and the Cup on an open-top bus and paraded us down Fifth Avenue. We had a band playing in the front of the bus, and the confetti and ticker tape swarmed down around us. It was a fantastic welcome. New York loved its tennis players that day.

I also learned later that this was not my only involvement with ticker tape. During my match with Cramm in the Interzone, there was a noticeable lull in business during the periods when the radio play-by-play was broadcast. The broadcast was not allotted all the time that Gottfried and I required, so it was forced to leave the air periodically. At last, it came back on for the duration when I was down 3-1 in the fifth. Apparently, for the balance of the match it was possible to discern an appreciable decline in business transactions. After the match sales picked up again and the stock volume soon reached its normal level.

When at last I found my way back to Oakland in the fall, the city honored me with a Don Budge Day. I was marched down Broadway, and the mayor welcomed the native son back with a speech and the presentation of a signet ring that featured the Oakland city seal, flanked by diamonds. My parents and the rest of the family and all my friends were with me. It was a glorious way to end 1937. The next year was the Grand Slam—and I was already envisioning it then—but in this year I had stopped traffic on Fifth Avenue, on Wall Street, and on Broadway, Oakland. Rod Laver was never able to manage that sweep too, even if he did eventually match my Grand Slam.

5

Friends and Foes

A champion is forever under tight scrutiny. If he cannot be beaten from off the top, there are always those ready to try to discredit him, so as to at least fault him during his stay there. This is easy, perhaps, because most people have a singular image of a champion and expect all to be of the same sort. I never understood that, nor did I agree with it. There is simply no such thing as prototype champion behavior, for an athlete rises to the top the way he is, and it is too late for him to conform to any preordained champion mold once he arrives.

Let's face it: I didn't become champion because I kept training; I kept training because that was the only way I could become champion. Believe me, I'm sure that if I could have made it without being so Spartan, I surely would have tried. I wasn't being noble; I was being expedient.

On only one strange occasion did I know I could play it up at night and not have my play on the court suffer. That happened at a pretty crucial time too—in 1938, at Forest Hills, when I was going for the last victory in the Grand Slam. I had to face Gene Mako in the finals. Gene and I had long been the closest of friends, and we were rooming together throughout the tournament at the Hotel Madison in Manhattan. Our finals match was on Sunday, but the famous hurricane of '38 was cranking up then, and it rained us out that day. The rain forced a postponement on Monday too, and both Gene and I started getting a little edgy. It was not just the tennis. Both of us had special girl friends in town, and we had been waiting patiently for the tournament to end so we could have a little more fun without worrying about conditioning.

Gene and I talked this over, and on Monday night we decided to go out, each his own way, and report back to the room at midnight. We were the only two guys left in the tournament, so as long as we knew what the other was up to, all was fair in love and war. We took our girls out Monday night, and checked each other in with Cinderella promptness at midnight. Tuesday, though, it rained again, and the weather forecast for the next few days was no better, so the Forest Hills officials decided to hold the finals off for a few more days, and plan it definitely for Saturday, when we could draw a large week-end crowd.

This development called for another serious confrontation between those two eager finalists, Mako and Budge. "Look Gene," I said, "we're still the only two guys involved in this. What do you say we make a motion that the curfew be extended till two?" The motion was made and the vote carried 2-0. So every night, then, the rest of the week, I would head off for an evening on the town with my girl, and Gene with his. We'd drop the girls off and check each other in at two. It was a very satisfactory arrangement, and while neither Gene nor myself went off on any sort of wild bacchanalian tear, Tommy Dorsey was in town—at the Astor or the New Yorker —and I trained for the finals mostly to his music.

Indeed, things were so agreeable for both of us that on Saturday morning, when the sun relented and came out for the finals, Gene and I didn't wake up early enough, and it wasn't till noon, just two hours before our match was to begin, that we both struggled out of bed. We dressed in a hurry and rushed down to the Golden Horn Armenian restaurant for some brunch. We made it to Forest Hills just in time to take the courts at two o'clock. Of course, if we had not, I don't know what would have happened. Does anybody know the procedure if both finalists fail to show on time? Do both forfeit and the semifinal losers, by default, play off? Or do you call it a draw, like a double knockout?

Well anyway, we *did* make it just under the wire, our brunches still rattling around in our stomachs, and I beat Gene in four sets to win the Grand Slam—and that old devil-may-care Budge managed the feat after a week of two o'clock nights under the bright Manhattan lights.

Of course there were a few real, honest-to-goodness party boys on tour. Invariably, it seemed, these players were ranked just outside the highest group of players. This always led everyone to say, "What a guy that Joe is! Stays up all night partying and can still play tennis. Just think how much better he would be if he kept training and really applied himself." It was always my impression, however, that the cause-and-effect relationship was not quite as it appeared. I always felt that these guys turned to more partying than playing because they found out they could not win, and not the other way around.

In my own case, as I matured and progressed to the top of the sport, I began to build my own model of exactly how *I* should act if I ever did find considerable success. I began to set up my own standards for championship demeanor almost from the first day that I won a tournament. Just as I established a philosophy of playing, so I also established one of behaving. This may all sound a bit dreamy, but the thought of being a champion was always with me, and it was only natural that I should devote some of my dreaming time to the matter of conduct. Early in my career one particular incident encouraged me to set up standards for myself.

I was playing in a junior tournament in Los Angeles and had finished for the day, so I was standing by the court watching the men's matches with a properly reverent awe. Playing on the court—a good old California concrete court—was a great Australian champion. (I'll let it go at that; I'd rather not name him.) He was up against a fairly nondescript opponent, but the fellow was on his game and beat him. Ellie Vines was standing there, very near me, and when the Australian moved off after the defeat, Vines tried to console him with a couple of kind words. The Aussie nodded to Vines for making the polite effort but otherwise just shrugged without interest. "Thanks, Ellie," he said, "but never mind. I would have beaten him if we'd played on grass or clay."

To measure my naïveté, I can say simply that I was utterly

shocked at such an attitude. I decided at that moment that if I were ever champion, I wanted to be champion of all surfaces and all climates and of Tuesdays as well as Saturdays. I think I held to that when I finally did become number one. And if I did, I believe I managed to because I prepared myself to lose without excuse at an early age.

Another thing that I decided early in my career was that I would not let up on an opponent. I found that no matter how slight the caliber of competition, I could not relax, for I possessed the type of game that could fall apart entirely in an instant and, like Humpty Dumpty, could not be put back together again. This was because of my style—the hard, driving, attacking game that demands a groove. I know that I came in for criticism on some occasions when I would not let up on someone that I had completely outclassed. I protested (usually without success) that my game was not the sort that could be turned on and off like a light switch. I also feel that a player compliments his opponent by refusing to let up on his game. To me, the player who does not maintain his game at the hilt, who teases a lesser opponent, is insulting the loser, even if the score appears "respectable."

However, this is hardly any sort of consensus opinion. Bobby Riggs succeeded me as champion after I turned pro, and Bobby was forever toying with his opponents. Riggs was a fairly good offensive player, with an underrated serve for the smaller man that he was. But his strength was defense. In that he was superlative, and even, I can tell you, infuriating at times. Completely opposite to me, Bob could raise and lower his game virtually at will. He could be most deceptive against a weaker man, playing with him until he finally decided, mercifully, to put the poor fellow out of his misery. Riggs was like a race horse that stays head and head, whatever the pace, and then takes off on his own whim and wins by ten lengths down the stretch. That was Bobby. Against someone whom he could obviously whip, his whole game was suddenly cat-and-mouse. He'd drop-shot, lob, lose interest (and a few games), slice, and spin— but always, always make it very obvious to all that he could win when he really wanted to. And then he would.

Even if I had wanted to have played that way, I couldn't have. Too much of my edge lay in power, and even, if you will, fear, whereas Riggs featured cunning and guile. Once I let an opponent think he had a chance in a match, I was really showing my hole card. Too often I have seen that once an underdog comes to believe that he might have a chance, he really does have a chance. I always felt that my chances increased the more that I could frighten an opponent. That was the way I approached each match. I guess it made me look like a redheaded ogre sometimes, but it was the only way I could survive. In fact, when the draw sheets were posted, the players would gather around to see "who's going to be fed to the Fire Dragon today." Incidentally, this epithet is the origin of the dragon insignia embroidered on the Don Budge line of tennis clothes made by McGregor Sportswear.

But when the draw was posted, I was never among those who rushed to see who their opponents were to be. "Hey, J.D.," a player would ask me, "who do you play?" I would say that I didn't know. I hadn't looked at the draw, and I didn't intend to. I feel that if I am to win the tournament, I have to be able to beat any comer, whether I meet the toughest contender in the first round or in the finals. I only worry about one match at a time. This approach may have stemmed from my first tournament, when I was fifteen and beat Phil Carlin, the number-one seed, in the first round, naïvely unaware that he had been picked to walk off with the trophy.

A corollary to this philosophy was to convince *myself* that I was invincible, and that was probably the more difficult task. To effect it, I could not let anything get the best of me. For instance, one day early in my career I won a good match, and the next day, when I came to the courts, I found myself studiously repeating my previous day's procedure. I had just about put the same shirt I had worn the day before over my head in the same manner I had put it on then, when I stopped myself. Now this, I said to myself, is ridiculous. The shirt didn't win and the shoes didn't win, and I am just not going to get involved with superstition.

Superstition was common among the players. Many of them often dressed in some very lucky—and very gamy—outfits. Shrewd as I thought I was, I developed so many habits to prevent me from becoming superstitious that I developed something of a reverse superstition. Only I think I called it discipline and let it pass proudly. For instance, if I finished a match and I had a blister on, say, my left foot, I would force myself to take the right shoe off first. No superstition for Budge.

That is a small thing to lead to a larger point—that tennis players, more than most other athletes, are left to their own devices. They must learn by experience and trial and error. It is, too, the rare young boy, faced with the pressures of the game, who can make a succession of right decisions without proper guidance. Everyone berates the young American players for their poor manners, and while I would not often dispute that generalization, I find, sadly, that their lapses are often the fault of the adults who are in charge. Too many of our adult tennis supervisors are too lenient with the youngsters.

Since tennis is, in the main, an individual sport, special conflicts can be quickly established when the players are suddenly asked to put team priorities first. And that is what happens with the Davis Cup. I think that part of the reason that the United States has fared so poorly in recent years is that a bunch of individuals spend too much Davis Cup time in search of a team. They have been poorly guided to this point, and the leadership on the team continues in this insipid vein. It is rare that a recent American captain has provided the level of leadership that Walter Pate, who was usually my captain, gave to us. The exception was Billy Talbert, but he lost the job because the tennis hierarchy felt that he was using the position of captain to improve his business contacts. Frankly, I could never see the crime in that, especially since Talbert was obviously capable of doing better at both his jobs than most of the captains were with only one.

Talbert, like Pate, was genuinely admired by the players. Also, both of these outstanding captains, each in his own way, led the enterprise with firm authority. Captain Pate made it clear to us that we were representing our families, our team, and our country and that everything must be directed to the collective effort. Further, he pointed out that if any player did not see fit to accept these terms, a return ticket home was to be the only way the conflict would be resolved. We developed a genuine camaraderie under Pate. We became, simply, a tennis *team*.

More than receiving direction from the captain, though, we also were provided with great precepts of leadership among the members themselves. The older players helped perpetuate a firm continuity that has, for the most part, recently been in evidence only on the great Australian squads. The older players set a pattern and passed it along. The classic case of the effects of our team spirit was largely responsible for my getting my first (and unexpected) opportunity to play in top-flight Davis Cup competition in 1935.

I had played earlier that year in the matches against China and Mexico—teams we completely outclassed. But when we came up next against Germany in the Interzone Finals at Wimbledon, I was consigned to the role of spear carrier. Sidney Wood and Wilmer Allison, the nation's two top-ranking players, were expected to play the singles, as they had the year before. I played well, though, and I was beating both of them regularly in practice. It was an unexpected development, and it left our captain, Joseph Weir, in a terribly difficult position. After all, I was hardly past my twentieth birthday, and I was ranked only ninth in the country.

Weir was in his room at our hotel a couple of nights before the matches with Germany began. He was to announce the team the next day. There was a knock on his door, and when he answered, there was Wood. Weir was a little surprised, but he immediately invited Sidney in, and he came inside. Sidney stood there, a bit self-consciously, shifting on his feet. "What is it, Sidney?" Weir asked.

"Oh, look, Cap," Wood said. "I've been thinking and thinking, and finally I just had to come over and say this. Look, I know it and you know it. Don has been playing well. He's been better than either Wilmer or me. I hate to say it, but I think you ought to replace me in the singles with Budge."

Weir sighed. "Sidney," he finally said. "Thank you. Just, thank you very much. You have made this a whole lot easier for me. I agree

with you, and I have known it, but I have just been agonizing with
myself whether I should make that decision. You've made it possible for me to."

Wood's sacrifice, it turned out, was more far-reaching, perhaps,
than he had imagined at that moment. I did replace him against the
Germans, and I won both my matches. Allison helped win the tie
for us by teaming with Van Ryn in the doubles victory and winning one of his singles matches. A couple of weeks later, however,
just before the Challenge Round against Great Britain began, Weir
found Wood rapping on his door again, and this time Sidney solic-
ited Weir to put him back in the line-up, though not for Budge, but
for Allison. Weir said only that he would consider the issue. He did,
but in the end, he finally decided against changing the team, and
Wood sat out the Challenge Round as well as the Interzone.
Thus it developed that the night Sidney walked in and suggested
that he be replaced in the Interzone was the time that his career in
major international competition ended.

Wood's sacrifice produced quite an extraordinary incident, and
I would not suggest that we all tended toward such selflessness. I
will say, however, that I do not believe that the attitude among today's players is on a par with that in our time. We had our soreheads,
of course. We had our embarrassing incidents. But, all in all, proper
conduct and good sportsmanship seemed to be more valued qualities
with my generation. I can never, for instance, forget the chagrin
and, really, the shame, that I felt when I was first called a bad sport.
That the man calling me that was Cramm, who was the very exem-
plar of good sportsmanship, made the charge even more crushing.

It was on my first visit to Wimbledon, the summer of '35, when
everything was falling so neatly in place for me. I was heady with
new success, and probably, naturally, a bit smug, though I was trying desperately to be properly modest and to create the right first
impression. On the afternoon that I beat Bunny Austin (and, you
will remember, waved to the Queen) to qualify for the semis against
Cramm, he sought me out, introduced himself, and asked if I would
care to chat for awhile and get to know each other. I was delighted
and flattered, and Gottfried and I left the crush of the crowd and

Gottfried Cramm and I at Wimbledon in July 1937, that
incredible month.

The 1936 Interzone Matches at the Germantown Cricket
Club in Philadelphia. The Australian doubles team was
Jack Crawford and Adrian Quist, in the shorts. The
interesting thing about this old picture was that the key shot
in the match was a short backhand smash that Gene Mako
hit into the net. This could be that very shot. *(U.S.L.T.A.)*

I receive the Sullivan Award for 1937. No other tennis
player has ever won it. *(Wide World)*

Bill Tilden, Ellie Vines, and Lester Stoefen were with me on my first pro tour overseas. Shortly after this picture was taken, the war forced us to leave England and return home.

The Army–Navy matches of
1945, this one on Guam. I'm
the holdout in long pants, and
my partner is Frankie Parker.
The Army team across the
net is Bobby Riggs and Wayne
Sabin. I still held the pro
title and Parker was the
United States amateur champion at this time, so we had
open tennis twenty-three
years before its time.

Just a little later, home to
peace and the Los Angeles
Tennis Club.

Alice Marble and I are introduced to Gottfried Cramm's old doubles partner, King Gustav of Sweden.

The guy playing bass is Jack Kramer, who played much better tennis. He was pro champion at this point, 1949.

Gene Mako and I on our way to the Wimbledon titles in 1937 and 1938. I wasn't to be back there to play for another thirty years. *(U.S.L.T.A.)*

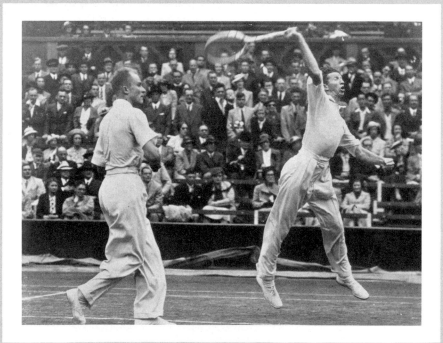

When I did get back to Wimbledon in 1968, John Faunce was my partner, after a technicality prevented Jack Kramer from playing. Faunce and I lost our second match in the Veterans' Doubles. Rod Laver *(below)*, the only other player ever to win the Grand Slam, took the first Open Wimbledon, and then Arthur Ashe, *(bottom)* triumphed in the first United States Open. There are many more good players now than there were when I was playing. *(Jerry Cooke, Sports Illustrated)*

In the summer I teach at my Don Budge Tennis Campus at McDonogh, Maryland, which is located outside of Baltimore. The lady is my wife Lori.

strolled over to an outside court. We found an empty bench there and sat down.

I was nervous, to be sure, determined to appear much more casual and mature than I could ever truly be in such company. Believe me, we all had great respect for Gottfried. He was easy, though, and I relaxed some, expecting no more than the pleasant sort of chit-chat I was sure he had in mind. So Cramm looked me squarely in the eye and began, "You know, Don, I watched your match today, and I must say I thought you were a very bad sport." I absolutely collapsed. I was not only crestfallen but genuinely confused, for I simply could not imagine what I had done in the match with Austin that Cramm could find unsportsmanlike.

"Look, Don," Gottfried began again, a bit more kindly, as he surely recognized my dismay. "We're going to play each other in two days, and I have the feeling that we're going to play each other a great deal more in the years ahead. I was perhaps too blunt, but I do think it is a good idea if we try to understand one another from the start." I nodded, still confused.

Then Gottfried called my attention to a point that had taken place in the third set, when the match was still very close. Austin had hit a good, hard shot past me, but the linesman had called the ball out. I thought the call was bad, and so, with a certain martyr's flair, I returned Austin's next serve directly into the net. I certainly remembered the point, because, specifically, I felt that my action was the very hallmark of good sportsmanship. Wasn't it?

"Absolutely not," Gottfried said. "You made a great show of giving away a point because you felt the call had wronged Bunny." I nodded. "But is that your right? You made yourself an official, which you are not, and in improperly assuming this duty so that you could correct things your way, you managed to embarrass that poor linesman in front of 18,000 people."

I don't believe I could even reply. That consideration was a revelation to me. I had always felt that I was being selfless and heroic in giving up a point to even up a bad call. I had never stopped to examine any other possible implications of my action. By the time our conversation ended, I had agreed sincerely that Cramm was right,

and I assured him that I would never again be guilty of such misplaced charity.

Ironically, in our semifinal match two days later, Gottfried got a
bad call in the very first game. I glanced up, a bit bashfully, toward
him. He wasn't even looking back, but was just moving in a busi-
nesslike way back to the service line. I played the next point to win
the game. When we crossed over, Cramm stopped for an instant,
and with just the touch of a wry smile, said, "I guess you do see
things my way." I didn't have time to reply and, as a matter of fact, I
don't recall that we ever even discussed the matter again.

In looking back, I think it was mainly Tilden's example that I
had been following. Bill was forever blowing points with grandeur,
if he had but the slightest notion that a linesman had erred on a
call. He was a master at a lot of things, and not least at such grand-
stand gestures. He would knock that next ball into the net, and you
could hear the crowd whispering bravos for his sportsmanship. Tilden could lose a point just as stylishly as he could win one.

Still, while it was not too irritating that he proceeded this way on
his own, the really annoying thing was that he never inquired about
how you felt on the subject. Tilden just assumed that his opponent
would be behaving in the same way at his end of the court whenever
such arbitrary duty called. Moreover, Tilden did not just restrict
himself to calling points at his end. He also put himself in charge of
deciding whether the balls he was hitting out at *your* end were being
called correctly. If you felt a shot of his had gone out and so did the
linesman and so did everybody in the house, and Tilden thought
the ball had been in, he just tacitly assumed that you would blow
the next shot to even things up. If you didn't, he made it plain to you
later that he was terribly disappointed at your lack of sportsmanship. Any protests on your part were met with pointed regrets that
your eyesight was so obviously becoming deficient.

Shortly after I signed a professional contract to tour with Ellsworth Vines, I met with Ellie. One of the first things he said was,
"Don, I hope you don't mind if we play the points the way they're
called."

"Ellie, that's the only way I play them," I said.

"Oh, thank God," he said. He was genuinely relieved. "I'm so glad to hear that. All of this time I've had to put up with Tilden, who's grandstanding on every call. And now Perry has started to do the same thing to some extent."

Playing as many matches as we did on the tour, night after night, there was bound to be—and there was—a predictable number of absolutely impossible decisions, but Ellie and I played every shot exactly as it was called, without sympathy, and we never had a single argument on the whole tour.

I get a little annoyed sometimes when I hear intemperate behavior being excused on the grounds that the player involved is such a good competitor. Too often in tennis, I think, we have somehow come around to equating a good competitor with an old-fashioned hothead. Whenever I hear that suggestion, I am reminded again of Joe DiMaggio. Is there any argument that DiMaggio was not a great competitor? I remember on one occasion when I went out to Yankee Stadium with Toots Shor, the stout restaurateur, to see the Yankees play. It was a game late in the season, in the midst of the pennant race, and Bob Feller was pitching for the Indians against the Yankees. It was a close, low-scoring game, and in a late inning DiMaggio reached third base. The next batter hit a hard ground ball, and Joe was trapped between third and home.

Toots and I were sitting in a box that was located down low, right along the third-base line, so we were right on top of the play. DiMaggio was yo-yoing back and forth in front of us, when the catcher took a toss from the third baseman and dropped the ball. Joe reversed his direction immediately and dived for the plate just as the catcher picked up the ball and tagged him. The umpire called, "Out."

DiMaggio raised up on his knees in the dust. "I was safe," he cried.

"Out," the umpire repeated. That was all. DiMaggio pulled himself up, dusted himself off, and jogged straight back to the dugout.

"He *must* have been safe," Shor said to me. "I've never seen Joe argue before." Argue? It was more reflex, like screaming "ouch" to a pinprick.

The point, I hope, is obvious for apologists for our tennis "competitors." The competitor in Joe DiMaggio caught the opening the instant the catcher dropped the ball. The competitor whirled and crashed for the plate. Then the competitor let the gentleman move to the fore. DiMaggio the gentleman accepted a tough—and probably bad—decision, one that had a bearing on a whole season's play. And he was no less a competitor for it. Tennis is a rugged, fast game, but it is, really, no less a game of inches and agony than any other sport. Competition is a fact of sport, and in tennis or any other game no one has a right ever to drag it up as an excuse for ill manners.

Of course, I do sympathize with the fact that because there is no contact in tennis, because the players are never permitted to take their frustrations out on each other, there is a seething pressure in a tennis player that needs an outlet. It is strange, though, that so little personal animosity ever appears on the court. Perhaps if tennis players could more often become genuinely angry at their opponents, just some of the pent-up frustration could find a more natural release. In my whole career, there was only one time that I was truly riled at an opponent, and my anger helped me win a match I had no business winning.

This occurred at the very end of my playing career, on the 1957 pro tour, when I was competing against Pancho Gonzales, Frank Sedgman, and Pancho Segura. I was forty-one then, and by all laws of geriatrics should have been mellowing. Or perhaps I was just turning into a crotchety old man. Anyway, I got mad as hell one night at Gonzales, and while it was over and done with by the next day, and while Pancho and I still play together as often as our schedules permit us to, he put me into a blue fury that night.

Pancho was the professional champion then, by all odds the best player in the world, and I had not been able to beat him once on this tour. When we came into his hometown, Los Angeles, he was truly at his determined and obstinate best. I know of no athlete who can conjure up better concentration and singlemindedness than Gonzales can. When he is playing, he can expel just about any other consideration from his mind. He would drive promoters crazy, for he would never participate in promotion, give interviews, or generally cooperate with the hoopla that was planned, after all, to bring more people into the arena and more money into his pocket. When he is concentrating on playing, he wants nothing to clutter his objective—winning.

So it was when we came into Los Angeles and the Olympic Auditorium. I was paired against him in the first night's action, and, serving easily, he took the first game of the match from me. I picked up the balls and began to make my first serve. The lighting in the Olympic was, to be generous, about the candlepower of a lovers' moon, and making out the opponent across the net, much less the ball, was a chore. In the gloaming, I noticed a scramble of photographers perched on the side of the court down by Pancho, hoping desperately to find enough light to catch a quick shot of him for the morning editions. I called down to them, asking them if they wanted to get a shot of Pancho making a return, and they yelled back anxiously that they would.

Stepping a bit inside the baseline, then, I lobbed a little serve to Pancho. He made a proper picture stroke back to me, the photographers took their shots, I took another ball, and prepared to make my first serve. But when I took up my position, I looked over and saw that Gonzales had moved over to receive in the other service court. At first I just assumed that he was kidding. But when I called down to him, all he did was shout back, "Come on, come on, serve."

"Hey, listen Pancho," I said. I still couldn't quite appreciate what he was up to. "That was just for the photographers. Go on back now. Come on."

He just shook his head at me, and maintained his posture, waiting for me to serve. He was being cute, but he was also absolutely determined to stand his ground. He had no intention of acknowledging that my serve for the cameras was anything less than real.

Stunned now, when at last I understood his mind, I gave up arguing with Pancho and began to plead with the umpire. "You *can't* believe I was really serving," I cried. "I wasn't even behind the baseline."

"Play, Mr. Budge," said the umpire.

"Call a foot-fault on me, then," I said.

"We are not calling foot-faults tonight, Mr. Budge."

"All right," I said, "in that case I'll serve from the service line."

"Come on, Mr. Budge," said the umpire, "let's play tennis. Love-fifteen."

"Are you going to play?" Gonzales called.

"I can't believe this," I said. Now I was getting mad.

"Don't be officious, Mr. Budge," the umpire said.

"Let's go, Budge," Gonzales called.

"You will have to serve, Mr. Budge," the umpire told me. "Love-fifteen."

I realized at last that neither one of them had any intention of listening to me. "If that's the way you're going to be, Pancho," I said, tight-lipped now. "If one lousy point—if you're that desperate. All right." I was absolutely seeing red now. I was never so determined to beat anyone in my life. If all the angels in heaven had been holding tennis rackets, staring at me from across the net along with Gonzales, I would have had no fear in taking the whole lot of them on.

I won my serve, and we held to 4-all, when I got him to a break point, 30-40. He smashed one of those perfect 118-m.p.h. jobs at me, but I somehow managed to get my backhand in front of it, and I passed him cold. I held my serve to take the set, and in the next set, I broke him again at 4-4, and held to take the match. It was hardly the most important win of my life, but it may have been the most satisfying. And for his part, Gonzales now turned as mad as I had been earlier. He stalked off the court and into the locker room and stomped right down on a new hundred-dollar suitcase he had just bought. His foot went right through it. If possible, that made him even madder.

As I was walking off the court, Pancho's father came out of the crowd and headed over to me. Mr. Gonzales is just a wonderful gentleman, and he was so gracious that he even made me feel bad for a moment. "You just played so well, Don," he said.

"Mr. Gonzales," I said, "if your son hadn't been such a ———"

and here I employed quite a few references to Pancho that are usually most unadvisable to use in the presence of a parent, "if he hadn't made me so damn mad, he would have won that match."

"I know," Mr. Gonzales replied quietly, still completely a gentleman. "I was embarrassed for him."

Jack Kramer, who was promoting the tour, came over to me. "Don," he said, smiling Cheshire-like, "if we could get you that mad every match, I have no doubt that you would win the whole tour in a breeze." I have no doubts about that myself whatsoever.

If Gonzales forced me to the peak of my rage, Fred Perry was the one player who was able to get my goat on a more regular, if less emotional, basis. This was particularly true when we were traveling together as pros, and constantly in company. I don't suppose I could say that Fred ever really infuriated me, but he certainly had the knack of irking me. He is a funny sort, Fred, a loner mostly, but one with a bright and incisive sense of humor. His is a quick wit and it could be caustic, particularly if things were not going well on the court. As soon as I began beating him regularly on our first tour, he took to calling me J. Donald God, and the thing that especially annoyed me was that he would never use that name unless there were some others around to hear it. He could be brutally sarcastic when the mood hit him.

But he could also be wonderfully delightful, and he still is. It is rather ironic, but with all the world to get lost in, I, from California, and Fred, from England, end up about fifty miles from each other every winter on the little island of Jamaica. I am part owner of the Montego Bay Racquet Club there, and Fred is the athletic director of the Runaway Bay Hotel, which is just a couple of coves away.

Perry could, when the spirit hit him, be the most engaging player of all on the court. He had the charismatic kind of personality that could attract the sympathy and affection of a whole crowd. I could sense it as a gallery began to feel with Perry, to laugh with him. For purposes of comparison, I would rate Frankie Parker as the direct antithesis among my contemporaries. Frankie came across as absolutely cold and unemotional, the original poker face. One time I was sitting with Groucho Marx in the stands, watching Parker play. It was at least a couple of sets, I think, before Frankie showed any signs of expression at all. He pursed his lips. "There's that Parker, hysterical again," Groucho said.

As a crowd pleaser, I think I was almost directly between the two extremes. I did exhibit a certain country-boy quality that appealed mostly to the British. They made a great to-do and were positively enthralled with the way I would exclaim "Oh boy!" in praise and exasperation when an opponent would make a good shot against me. No one in America found the exclamation very interesting, but the British thought it so disarming of me—which, I suppose, is another reason they were so prepared to believe that I had waved how-de-do to the Queen. Anyway, I never had the stage presence of Perry or Tilden.

Fred, being British, had a special lien on Wimbledon, but I still cannot believe that there are many athletes, or actors, for that matter, who could command an audience the way he did for a few minutes in the middle of our 1936 semifinal. It was a close match at the start, and we split the first two sets, so for a while, every point was most important. Nevertheless, during one exchange, a piece of newspaper suddenly came drifting down out of the stands. Fred had only to make an easy return to win the point, but somehow the errant paper caught his attention and his fancy. He paused almost in mid-shot, neglected to even play the ball, and, instead, watched attentively as the paper wafted to the ground. The crowd watched, as confused as it was stunned.

Then, in a rather leisurely fashion, Fred walked over a few steps to where the paper had landed. Calmly and deliberately, he reached down for the paper, scanned it, and then began to read it in earnest.

I think that I was as spellbound by the action as any other of the 18,000 on hand. Fred himself remained unperturbed. After reading for awhile, he began to chuckle. The crowd, still bewildered, but warming to the stunt, began to laugh with him. And so did I. Then Fred proceeded to fall into an even deeper laugh, slapping his sides, guffawing, holding his stomach, absolutely roaring with delight at whatever it was that he was reading. Out of the stands, a whole cascade of deeper laughter rolled down, joining with his.

Well, since I was just as curious as anyone, and since I was also the one person in the whole place who was in a position to find out what was so funny, I rushed up eagerly as soon as he finally beckoned me to the net. As I neared, Fred just glanced up and quickly gave me a little wink. "Hey, what's so funny?" I asked.

"Nothing at all," he said, showing me the piece of paper. I think it had something as humorous as the weather report or the stock tables printed on it. "Laugh," he ordered me, out of the side of his mouth.

And so I did. I joined the act and started roaring myself. Fred resumed his belly-laugh, and we stood there at the net, in the midst of the semifinals at Wimbledon, chuckling like hyenas. By now, the whole of Wimbledon was in a panic. Then, promptly, with the timing of a real comedian, Fred abruptly decided to ring the curtain down on this number. He suddenly stopped laughing, folded up the paper neatly, put it in his back pocket, and strode purposefully back to serve. His spur-of-the-moment whim satisfied, Perry played the next point as violently as if nothing at all peculiar had preceded it. And I did too. We had our laugh and just went right back to the semifinals. I think there is a lesson there too in the matter of managing the competitive instincts.

Of course, I will grant that that sort of incident was the absolute extreme. It was, in fact, rare that I ever so much as exchanged a "nice day" with an opponent during a match, even when we were toweling off between games. It is too distracting to get involved in even the minimum of conversation. I also always found it unnecessary to start commiserating with an opponent who was losing. I just never saw the value in saying "too bad" or "tough luck" or other sentiments of that sort when the opponent missed a tough shot or hit a double fault or fell into any such sort of misfortune.

First of all, it is rather hypocritical to make such expressions, however sympathetic or friendly you might be with the other player. It can also be patronizing and even annoying if the two of you feel that you must try to outdo each other in offering condolences. Like giving away points, such expressions are most often a form of fraudulent, false sportsmanship.

Of course, there are masters of court repartee everywhere, even

in the world class, and a few chosen words, carefully selected, can
be an effective instrument of gamesmanship. For a classic case, I
would have to turn to Tilden again, although in this event he was
the surprised victim. Since Tilden was an impressive purveyor of
court con, and he used to tell this story on himself, this particular
ploy used against him must have truly been effective. It took place in
Paris in a Challenge Round match in 1929 when Tilden was facing
Jean Borotra of France, one of the famous Four Musketeers.

The action started after the very first game of the match, when
the two were changing sides. Borotra sidled up to Tilden. "Oh, beeg
Beel," he cried, looking up to the tall man with pointed respect.
"The forehand down ze line you have today. She is *magnifique!* She
is beautiful! How can I even stay in ze match wiz you today wiz a
forehand like that? Beautiful!"

Tilden smiled politely and went back out to play, but the next
time they crossed over, two games later, Borotra was at him again,
waxing even more enthusiastic. "Beel," he sighed. "Ohh, ze forehand. Better still. Down the line—ahh! Then you go wiz ze cross-
court, and I cannot do a thing. Today, wiz a forehand like that, I
will be grateful if I can even give you, a how-you-say, a sweat-up,
eh?"

This time, Tilden began to get the drift, and grew wary quickly
in the face of such uncompromising adulation, but as he moved back
out on the court, he could not help but be pleased with the reaction
that his forehand was creating. And he had no chance to forget,
either, for every two games, Borotra was back at him with more and
better compliments. Before long, as Tilden used to relate the story,
he was trying desperately to assist Borotra's good judgment by
placing more crisp forehands down the line. After a bit, he was trying, practically, to put his forehands *on* the line. Unfortunately, they
were falling out, and Borotra took the lead in the match. The Frenchman won the first set 6-4, and the crowd at Roland Garros was beside itself in anticipation of an upset. If Borotra could take this
match, France, with a 2-1 lead already, would have clinched the Cup
again.

Finally, to escape Borotra's siren call, Tilden said he started changing courts by going around the other end of the net from where Borotra crossed over. The Frenchman took quick note of this, and next time went to that side himself, pausing only to throw more bouquets to Big Bill each time they passed.

Next, in rising exasperation, Tilden tried to outwait Borotra. He would wait to see which side Borotra would head to at the end of an odd game, then he would go the other way. That defense had no chance to work, for Borotra, on his home grounds, could counter the strategy simply by outwaiting Tilden. Then, as always, he would rave on again about Tilden's forehand, and Tilden, moved despite himself, could not help but try to live up to Borotra's praise by clicking off a few more exquisite forehands. And too often, the shots would fall out.

At last, in complete desperation, Tilden chose the only option left him. To cross over, he strode right to the center of the net and scissored over it. Borotra apparently had neither the inclination nor the long legs to carry his policy to that extreme, and let the matter drop. Tilden, able to concentrate at last, settled down and won the match by taking the next three sets.

I never personally encountered such diabolical strategy, but on one occasion I did border a little on the devilish myself. In 1955, on the pro tour in Belgium, Pancho Segura and I fell into one of those silly shouting matches, where we were both pretending to be mad at each other. He called me a bum; I called him a stiff. I don't recall what provoked all the screaming, but we were enjoying ourselves, trying to top each other with outrageous braggadocio and impossible claims. We were also scheduled to play each other the next day, and so, as a parting shot, I yelled at Segura that he would see who was the boss soon enough—I would not give him the chance to hit even a half-dozen of his famous two-hand forehands when we played. He roared his disgust at my big talk.

But the next day, when we went on court, I was still determined to keep the ball away from Segura's forehand, and I played the whole match that way. I don't know if any of the fans realized the peculiar nature of the match, but I was able to let Pancho hit only five forehands all day. Not only that, but three of the forehands that

he did hit, he smashed out. I guess by the time he finally got a forehand, he was too anxious to know how to handle it. Or to remember.

I beat him 6-3, 6-2, but it was most unusual tennis. Since my
major effort was devoted to placement and this strategy stripped
Pancho of his powerful forehand, the match turned into a baseline
contest of accuracy, and the seventeen simple games took a full two
hours to play. It was a rewarding triumph for stubbornness.

6

The Grand Slam—My Favorite Invention

Except for a fluke, I might not have been the first person to win the Grand Slam of tennis. Jack Crawford of Australia really deserved to have accomplished that in 1933, five years before I did. Of course, it is also another fact that when Crawford almost managed the feat in 1933, and even when I *was* successful in 1938, no one was really aware that there was such a thing as the Grand Slam. If that sounds like I am saying Crawford almost won something that didn't exist anyway, I am. I take a certain whimsical pride in not only having won the Grand Slam but, in a sense, having created it as well.

The Grand Slam (or what has become known as the Grand Slam) entails winning the national singles championships of Australia, France, Great Britain, and the United States, the four major titles in the world, in one year. This designation was not arrived at arbitrarily, for these four nations were in 1938, and still are, the only countries to have won the Davis Cup. Indeed, only six other nations have even reached the finals, the Challenge Round: Italy and Spain, twice each; and Belgium, Japan, Mexico, and India, one time apiece. Other national championships—the Italian, particularly—have come to possess considerable international prestige, but the greater stature and tradition continue to lie only with the championships of the four nations that have won the Davis Cup.

By 1938, however, no one had thought to lump the four titles together as a Grand Slam, or as anything, for that matter. In those prewar days of primitive air travel, no one could quite conceive of a cluster of championships that had to stretch more than 10,000 miles to find all its members. If you look back upon press accounts at the time when I won Forest Hills to complete this far-flung cycle, you will find no reference whatsoever to my having won a "Grand Slam." Indeed, there was only passing note made of the fact that I had also won three other major national titles that year. For further commentary on the accomplishment, I think it is interesting that I was *not* presented the Sullivan Award in 1938, although I had won it in 1937, when I had taken only half of the Grand Slam. (I did repeat as the American Sportswriters' Athlete of the Year, an accolade I still cherish particularly. Byron Nelson, who won it in 1944-1945, and I remain the only back-to-back winners of this award, and I am the only tennis player ever to have been named for it.)

The fact that the Grand Slam was not recognized at the time is not unusual. Things of this sort tend to be accepted only with time and publicity. There was little special attention given when Babe Ruth hit sixty homers in 1927, and, similarly, the first horses to win the Kentucky Derby, Preakness, and Belmont in the same year were not acclaimed as Triple Crown winners. Bobby Jones figured out his own Grand Slam in golf before me—the amateur and open championships of Britain and the United States.

Conceivably, the fact that there was no such acknowledged entity as the "Grand Slam" made it somewhat easier for me. I was certainly not faced with the cumulative pressure of the press and the fans that Rod Laver had forced upon him when he took the Grand Slam in 1962, or that Lew Hoad faced when he came within a set of winning the four titles in 1958. For the athlete, however, pressure more truly comes from within, and so I doubt that my feelings and fears were any less intense than Laver's or Hoad's were a quarter of a century later when the full glare of world-wide publicity was upon them.

I had set my goal to win those four titles in 1938, and the fact that only Gene Mako was also aware of this made the accomplishment no less easy for me. Whether or not anybody else knew what I was trying to do, *I* did, and that is all that matters once you are on the court or any competition begins. Mako happened to end up as my opponent in the finals at Forest Hills, and there is irony in that, perhaps, but I doubt that his presence across the net served to make the matter any more trying. The pressure within me was full and sufficient enough, and whoever I had played and whether the newspapers or the fans knew could not have increased the pressure any.

It is curious, though, that while I won the Grand Slam without acknowledgment, the feat eventually caught the public fancy, and it remains the one thing I am most remembered for. I was delighted for Rod Laver when he too eventually won the Grand Slam, and I do hope that whatever developments tennis undergoes in the next important few years, the challenge and prestige of the Grand Slam will not be altered.

Of course, as I said, I should have been joining Crawford when I swept the four titles in '38. Jack had come to Forest Hills with the three other championships already won. Furthermore, he then gained his way to the finals against Fred Perry, and just as Hoad was to do twenty-five years later against Ken Rosewall, Crawford took a 2-1 lead in sets. He, not Perry, was still the world's premier amateur, and since he was ahead and playing comfortably, he should have been expected to go on and take the last set, for the United States title and for the first Grand Slam.

As I have mentioned, though, Jack was asthmatic, and particularly on the hotter, muggier days—as this one was—the condition could begin to bother him. To help his breathing in these circumstances, Crawford would often take a bracing shot of brandy before a match, or, if conditions warranted it, even in the midst of one. Against Perry and, no doubt, also against a high autumnal pollen count, frankly, Crawford started hitting the brandy too hard. He had two or three ponies, and his coordination began to suffer. Fred, cold sober, lost only one game to Crawford in the last two sets, and thus ended his chances for the first Grand Slam.

So it was that no one had ever won the four major titles in a single year, when I set out on my quest in 1938. Even so, the Grand Slam was never more than an auxiliary goal for me. My prime target was the Davis Cup, which we had finally won in 1937 and were defending on our home soil for the first time since 1927. It was for this reason that I turned down the first substantial pro offer that I was tendered in 1937. Then, as something of an afterthought, the Grand Slam occurred to me. The defending Davis Cup titlist does not have to qualify for the Challenge Round—it wins the right to defense automatically. It left my schedule greatly reduced, so I decided to shoot for the Slam as a way of staying competitively fit.

As I said, I told no one of my aims except Mako. I was top-ranked in the world, so I was certainly not going to be able to surprise anyone wherever I played, but I realized that if I did shout my intentions abroad, it would just make everyone want to get me with even greater intensity.

Although I did not require any reinforcement to this reasoning, Ellie Vines provided it anyway. I did not tell Ellie of my full design, but I did let him know that I was going to play in Australia before that fact was released. Vines had played there himself as an amateur and was immediately appalled that I was going. Citing his own experience, he begged me not to make the trip. "Don, please," he said, "don't go down there. It's so very seldom that they get our top players, and with the novelty of having the number one in the U.S. *and* the world, they will absolutely play you to death. That's what they did to me. You may win the Australian title, but I promise you, you'll pay for it later. *I* did and I know. You'll be so tired for the Challenge Round and for Forest Hills and maybe even by Wimbledon that you'll be lucky to do half as well as you'd do otherwise."

Even if he had not been so emphatic, I recognized that Vines had a good point. Quite aside from the simple esthetic value of winning the Davis Cup and Forest Hills was the obvious cold truth that poor performance late in the year stood to cost me a great deal of money if I decided to turn pro then. And if all went well, that was my hope, to turn pro.

It was difficult to argue with Ellie because I did not want to disclose to him that I was after the Australian title only as the first down card to a straight flush. But his advice was invaluable and convinced me that I could not poop myself out in matches that were mostly exhibitions to please the Aussie fans. I had to evaluate what

I thought was important for myself in terms of my long-range goal, so I devised a strict battle plan, with intentions to point for only two tournaments—the Victorian, which was scheduled shortly after I arrived in December '37, and the Australian National Championships themselves, about a month later. In this regard too, I took only Mako into my confidence.

I realized that I had gotten a great psychological boost the first time that I beat Cramm and the first time that I beat Perry when they had slacked off against me in what seemed to them to be unimportant matches. I realized that some younger player who stood in awe of me now could turn into a confident and real contender if ever he beat me once and showed himself that he could do it. But I figured that was the risk I had to take. It was a matter of priorities, and I wanted the Slam.

Gene and I sailed from San Francisco in the winter and soon were in the summer of the South Pacific. We worked very hard on that cruise at doing nothing. It was a twenty-one-day trip (twenty-three coming back the wrong way over the International Date Line), and we were well rested and sunburned when we arrived in Sydney. We still had a week to get our tennis legs back before the Victorian championships began in Melbourne. When at last they opened, I was truly eager to play tennis. I swept the tournament without the loss of a set.

Then I fell into a comfortable possum posture. I had agreed to play several exhibitions and some test matches (with Gene) that were run along the Davis Cup format. I was beaten regularly in these matches. I approached every match as if it were practice. Physically, I did not extend myself, and rather than do what was strategically wisest, I often tried to work on the facets of my game that I felt needed most attention. The Australian press was at first encouraged that the local boys had begun to turn the tables on Budge, but the writers became, perhaps, a little suspicious of my repeated failures as time wore on. Besides, the issue of my health had to be inserted for a time, for I suddenly lost my voice and went for several days without being able to say a word. I felt fine otherwise, though, and the doctors were unable to locate any other signs of a more serious illness.

By the time the National Championships began, my speech had returned as mysteriously as it had gone, and I was so eager to play in earnest that I could hardly conceal the method in my madness. I was like a loosed tiger after the first ball that bounced. I was relaxed and tough, perfectly tuned for the action, and I swept through the field with ease. I played John Bromwich, who was the coming Australian player, in the finals, and I beat John badly—6-4, 6-2, 6-1. Then, as quickly as possible afterwards, barely after the trophies had been presented, Gene and I were on the boat home, lounging in the deck chairs and watching the Southern Hemisphere roll by.

France was next, in May. I had been there only once before, two years earlier, to play in an international match of no real signifi-cance, so Paris and all its beauty in that last peacetime year was really new to me. Gene and I stayed at the old Hotel Majestic, which is on the Avenue Kleber, just off the Champs Élysées near the Arc de Triomphe. The Majestic is a grand old Victorian hotel, a wonderful residence for us, though it has since become more of a political monument. The French Ministry of Information had its headquarters placed there after hostilities broke out, and when the Germans moved into Paris, the Gestapo became the new tenants. In 1968, of course, the Majestic became the site of the Vietnam peace talks.

This was all before us then, though, and Gene and I did not even have the time to concern ourselves with the usual temptations of Paris in the springtime, considerable as they were. Our main problem was something of a much more prosaic nature—adjusting to the en tout cas courts, which are surfaced with packed dust made of crushed red brick. The French championships at the Roland Gar-ros courts is the only competition of the four Grand Slam titles that is not contested on grass.

We had begun preparing for the en tout cas back in the States by stopping off for a week or so in New York and practicing on the clay courts at Forest Hills before embarking for Europe. Before that I had rested at home for several weeks after returning from Australia, for I was wary of burning myself out, particularly as I had never played seriously so early in the year.

Truthfully, that concerned me more than the switch to clay, for the fact that I had won most of my recent important victories on grass was somewhat deceptive. Clay hardly frightened me. After all, I had learned the game on those gravel courts of Oakland that were much more similar to clay than to grass.

The French championship was the least memorable of the four in my Grand Slam. The tennis was not very exciting, and besides, I had terrible diarrhea during the whole tournament. My most pleasant memory was of Pablo Casals, whom I met and came to know so well during the tournament. I remember him much more than the tennis.

Despite my malady, I encountered serious competition only once, in the quarter-finals, when a Yugoslavian left-hander named Franjo Kukulevich took two sets from me. But he never gained the lead, and I never felt threatened seriously. I was fighting myself and my own very bad tennis that day more than I was the Yugoslav. I also have clear recollection of signaling to a friend in the stands, Russell Kingman, beckoning him to bring me something to eat. This went on throughout the tournament. I always came up hungry at the wrong time, and if Russell hadn't been on hand to smuggle candy bars and sandwiches out to me as I played, I might have collapsed at some point.

By the day of the finals, June 11, the diarrhea was almost gone and I was beginning to feel better. Roderich Menzel of Czechoslovakia was my opponent. He was a huge man, the tallest of my contemporaries. He stood about six four and weighed well over 200 pounds. (And remember, this was still a time when I, at six one and a half, was considered quite tall. I had filled out some by now to about 155 pounds, though I was temporarily lighter because of my stomach problems at this particular time.) Menzel was a fine player, and I considered him the best clay-court player in the world after Cramm, and Gottfried, whom I had expected to be playing against this last day at Roland Garros, was now in a jail somewhere in Germany. We had said good-by in Australia, but the Nazis arrested him upon his return on March 4, and just a few days before we docked at Cherbourg, on May 18, Cramm was convicted on outlandish charges and thrown in jail.

I was not surprised by then. It was obvious that they intended to embarrass and punish Cramm for his failure to turn Nazi. A few weeks before, early in May, I had headed an appeal that was directed in the form of an open letter addressed to the Nazi hierarchy. I had helped assemble twenty-five sports figures, including such people as DiMaggio and Alice Marble, and together we signed a message, entreating the Nazis to withdraw the false charges against Cramm and let him return to the tennis courts.

In the letter, we wrote that Baron Gottfried von Cramm was the "ideal sportsman, a perfect gentleman and decency personified. . . . No country could have wished for a finer representative—no sport for a more creditable exponent." The plea, as we all feared, was of no avail. He was in jail when I would surely have been playing him for the clay-court championship at Roland Garros in June; he was in jail until that October.

It was in Paris, on the clay, where I am sure Gottfried would have been at his formidable best. Menzel was the best on this surface after Cramm, but no fair substitute really, and he provided neither the drama nor the competition in the finals that Gottfried surely would have. I defeated Roderich without incident, 6-3, 6-2, 6-4, in less than an hour.

I remember that evening with much more clarity and pleasure than I do the afternoon. Russell Kingman had introduced me to Señor Casals earlier, and Pablo became a faithful visitor to the courts and a special fan of mine. "If you win, Don," he told me halfway through the tournament, "I would like to give a concert in your honor."

He did not forget the promise, and the party was held at Pablo's own apartment. It was a glorious setting, the city bright as ever below, the Eiffel Tower visible through the picture window, dominating the beautiful Paris night. As the songs say, we all remember Paris. I remember it that way, from Pablo's atelier, the night I won my French title. We assembled in the living room after dinner, and sat on large, magnificently ornate and comfortable cushions on the floor. Pablo and the pianist he had brought in to accompany him moved to their instruments. He took his cello, and then, just before he began to play, he paused and said, very simply, "This concert is for my good friend Don Budge." That was all. I don't believe I was ever so flattered.

Mr. Casals played for me for almost two hours—considerably longer than I had been on the court that afternoon. I can remember recounting the incident later to a rather surprised Benny Goodman. "Don," he said at last, "do you know there are some people who would pay $50,000 for just such an evening?" I nodded humbly. By that standard, the French title was worth more than any other championship in tennis history. There was certainly no better way to leave Paris either, and the memory, however priceless, would have been worth even more to me had we known something of what was ahead. I would not be back in Paris until a war and a decade had passed over its streets. It was the eve of my twenty-third birthday when I left.

Wimbledon was next, and it was to be a curious tournament for me. I came to it after an easy triumph at Queens, a warm-up that helped me readjust to the grass. I was in good shape and top spirits—as it turned out, I was on my way to winning twenty-seven straight matches abroad—and I felt that my chances to repeat were excellent. By midway in the tournament, however, this buoyancy had been replaced by despair because for the first and only time in my career, my backhand was giving me trouble. It was inconsistent, and I had lost faith in it. I was becoming sure that, of all things, my backhand would cost me the Grand Slam.

Paradoxically, though, after falling to these depths, I was not only able to restore my backhand but to finish the tournament with a victory over Bunny Austin when I exhibited as fine a game of tennis as perhaps I ever showed as an amateur. And I owed it all to some grand old lady whose name I never knew, whom I never actually met, and whom I saw only once. But she was playing tennis then, and that old gal could hit a helluva dandy topspin backhand.

My own backhand, as I have indicated before, was derived naturally from baseball. I had a free, easy swing, and depending on the situation, it was as accommodating for me to hit up on the ball as down under it. It was just natural, and so I imagine the facility must have come from learning to swing a baseball bat differently according to where a ball was pitched.

Today, few players even try to hit different types of backhands. The backhand appears to have been relegated to being a strictly defensive shot. The backhand is almost invariably now hit with underspin, the stroke beginning high and finishing low. If we continue the tennis-baseball analogy this is comparable to the kind of swing a ballplayer makes when he is trying to punch an outside pitch for a single, or just to move the runner along with a ground ball. Try it with a bat and a racket, and you will see.

When I was playing, there were many more of us who hit an offensive backhand, the stroke beginning down low, ending up high, with topspin and the flourish of a home-run hitter. There is nothing very tricky to this. Since you hit the ball with a squared-up face and don't have to concern yourself with beveling it, it may, in fact, be an *easier* backhand to hit than the underspin variety. I certainly cannot suggest that it is all a vanishing art. It just seems to me that confidence in the backhand is gone. Players today have so little faith in their backhand that they would rather hit down under it and use it to parry. They figure they can thrust later with a forehand or a volley.

Of all the modern players, I think Manuel Santana of Spain and Arthur Ashe hit the most devastating offensive topspin backhands. Of the pros, Rosewall hits the best backhand, but he always uses underspin, beginning the stroke high. Although Ken uses only that one type of backhand, he has the amazing ability to hit the ball so hard that he can regularly turn on terrific power (they call the little fellow "Muscles") and change a normally defensive shot into an offensive one. Two other professionals, Laver and Dennis Ralston, employ topspin, unlike Rosewall, but neither does it so well as either Ashe or Santana, in my opinion.

Of my contemporaries, Don McNeill hit perhaps the best offensive topspin backhand. It was a prime reason for his upset victory in the finals of Forest Hills in 1940, when he beat Bobby

Riggs. That defeat cost Riggs the honor of being the only player in the twentieth century besides Tilden to win the United States title three straight times. Riggs had a pretty fair topspin backhand himself, although it was not the equal of McNeill's, or of Frank Kovacs's or Parker's. Tony Trabert was one player who had a reliable attacking backhand in the 1950s. Even by then, though, the stroke was becoming almost exclusively a defensive instrument, and the usage of the topspin backhand was fading rapidly.

Despite all those superb backhands, from Parker to Ashe, I would settle for none but my own. I state that unequivocally, not because I think mine was necessarily better but because I am sure that it was a more natural shot than anyone else's. Tom Stow changed various parts of every other aspect of my game, but he never tampered with the backhand. He has always taught his students to swing as I did. I still hear people comment that my backhand looks so different. It is, I suppose. It is just so simple.

Indeed, in the case of explaining how to hit a backhand as I do, I do not want to go into a long involved polemic on exactly how and when to pivot your hips and turn your shoulders and swivel your neck and furrow your brow and so forth and so on. If you will hit the easy baseball-style backhand that I do, about all I must tell you is to stand sideways, feet spaced comfortably apart, and then stroke through the ball—that is, do not flail at it like a .050-hitting pitcher. If you follow my suggestions, the rest of your body, the legs and the shoulders and the arms and the back, will all take care of themselves. You will be surprised how easy it is to hit a really good backhand.

For the best backhand grip, I advise turning the hand about a one-eighth turn farther behind the racket than with the forehand— and remember the forehand is the shake-hands, flat part of the hand upon the flat part of the racket. Turn your hand the one-eighth turn and you are ready for the backhand.

My backhand grip is, incidentally, exactly the same one as the Continental *forehand* that was used by such players as Perry, Cochet, and Drobny, except that I put my thumb diagonally up behind the back of the handle. The Continental forehand is turned the other way from the western, and is thus best for reaching low balls, and is most vulnerable to high bounces. (See page 57 for grips.) I always felt that the reason Fred Perry could manage so well with the Continental forehand grip was because he had such a strong, massive wrist. He could handle stress in reaching for high balls that other players could not.

The backhand shot should begin with your elbow in tight to your body—which is, again, the example of most sound baseball batters. When you move up on your toes in preparation to swing, the elbow will move out from your body, so that you will be uncoiling with power. Follow through directly and without waste motion. The left arm should be brought back with the racket. Remember, I began as a two-handed hitter, and I actually gripped the racket handle with my left hand. The motion is the same with the proper one-hand swing. As the racket goes forward to hit the ball, you "release" your left hand and let it go out naturally behind you. You should look a bit as though you are trying to fly as you go into the follow-through.

Although I would be delighted to see the topspin backhand return to fashion, I want to repeat that I often had occasion to hit the defensive underspin backhand (high to low) when strategy dictated. The swing is the same, except that you are bringing the racket down, and you must bevel it slightly—about the angle of a three- or four-iron, if you are familiar with golf—for you are swinging down, in league with gravity, and you simply must hit somewhat under the ball if it is to clear the net.

If you also want to hit an offensive backhand—and I hope that you do—you will discover that you can make the shot by hitting it with a flat racket face, starting your backswing low and finishing up high. Remember, the offensive backhand is up, the defensive down. Swinging up on the offensive backhand imparts sufficient topspin, I have found, so that the ball can clear the net by quite a bit and still have the spin on it to fall inside the baseline.

The player with the telling offensive backhand is always a special threat simply because his talents have become so rare. Tennis strategy on so many levels now consists almost entirely of the one ploy: *Play to the backhand.* I'll bet that every time you face a new opponent, and whatever your caliber of play, your first thought is to work to his backhand. And he is just as quick to start working on yours. The player who develops a respectable backhand that can actually make points has a dual advantage.

First, a backhand gives you an all-court game. How many players are really vulnerable for a whole *half* of the court? It is like failing to bring a putter along when you play a round of golf. But further, the extra dividend a good backhand supplies is the element of shock. The assumption that it is always safe to play to the backhand is so widely held and is also so generally accurate that when a player runs into an opponent who renders that bias false, he is thrown into confusion and obstinacy. The play-his-backhand strategy is so ingrained that people will continue to try it long after they actually realize that their opponent really is strong on that side.

It was rare, too, that my backhand ever disappointed me. When I was good, it was very good; when I was bad, it was still good. You can imagine, then, the utter despair I was thrown into at Wimbledon when I finally realized that my backhand had gone off for the first time. I knew it had to cost me a match soon.

I was also at a complete loss to understand why my best shot was suddenly so inconsistent. I would hit two or three pretty fair backhands in a row, and then I would get a chance to turn one into a real winner, and that's when my reliable backhand would leave me. The more this happened, the more I fretted, and the worse I became. Moreover, at just about this time I suddenly developed the curious throat difficulties I had experienced in Australia in January, and I began having trouble speaking again.

Altogether, I became quite convinced that I would lose my next match in the quarter-finals. Feeling sorry for myself, and also trying desperately to understand what was wrong with my game, I left the hurly-burly of the players' area late one afternoon and wandered off by myself. I had no idea where I was headed, and just meandered along, turning this way and that among the pathways that wind between the many outside courts.

At last I found myself far out, alongside something like Court 32. It was late in the day, the big matches had ended, and out here where I had ended up I was the gallery of one for what I think was a Ladies' Veterans' Singles match. I was not really watching the two women play, just sort of staring at them absent-mindedly, seeing through them, really, to wherever my mind was. One of the ladies was dominating the match, though—that must have been obvious—and without knowing it I began to follow her more closely. Then I realized that I was concentrating on her. Slowly it began to dawn on me that some part of me quite below my conscious was being impressed. It was all curious, and I began to watch her more carefully.

Suddenly it was there. That old girl moved over and reached out and hit this gorgeous zinging topspin backhand. I kept watching. She did it again, and the rest just all fell into place for me. *She* was hitting a topspin backhand the way you are supposed to, stroking up; *I* had stopped hitting mine that way. I was trying to hit all my backhands with underspin. It was all, quickly, very, very plain before me. I saluted the lady, my benefactress, and dashed off to the clubhouse. Bitsy Grant, the poor fellow, was just putting his clothes on when I arrived.

"Come on, Bitsy," I said, "you've got to give me a hit."

"Don," he protested. "Not now. It's late. We can get a good long one in tomorrow."

"Please," I said. "I've got to play right now with someone. I think I just found out what I've been doing wrong with my backhand, and I won't even be able to sleep tonight if I don't try it out now."

Grant cocked a tired eye at me, realized I was serious, and shook his head. He stopped buttoning his shirt in mid-button and began unbuttoning. I was in my tennis whites as quickly as I could rush into them, and I hustled Bitsy out to a sidecourt. "Just hit them all to my backhand," I yelled at him, and he started feeding ball after ball to my left. He was a good sport. I hope I remembered to buy him dinner.

It took hardly any time at all for me to see that my guess was right. I had not been hitting my offensive backhand. I had been using my defensive swing, stroking from high to low, on all my backhand shots. Not only that, but I believe I had been hitting that shot sloppily too by beveling the racket too much. I have no idea where I had lost the touch or how long it had taken to fade from me, but I know I was back in the groove within the few minutes I hit with Grant.

Once I had my backhand again, I was like Peter Pan getting his shadow back—a great deal more grateful for it than I had ever been before. I moved right back into peak form again and rushed through to a finals match against Austin. Except for the first two games there was little contest to it, which is unfortunate because it was the last time that Bunny and I ever met, and the scores of this final meeting —6-1, 6-0, 6-3—were certainly not representative of the closer matches we had usually played against each other.

It was just one of those days when I could do no wrong, and it was my good fortune that such a performance should fall in the finals of the most important tournament in the world. Bunny's best chance came in the opening game, which, as it turned out, was the longest and most thrilling of the match. He had three chances to break my serve, but lost each of the break points, and at last I held after five deuces. Bunny came right back to sweep me at love in the next game, so that it is possible to imagine such a lopsided match as this one having taken on a different flavor if Bunny, the underdog, had broken me in that first game and jumped off on top.

As it was, though, the competition was through after the first two games. I held my serve and broke him twice in a row to take the set 6-1. I won the next set at love and swept to a 3-0 lead in the last set before at last he broke me. I had won fourteen straight games, leading with my backhand, constantly attacking with it.

I broke Bunny seven consecutive games during this stretch, but each one of the breaks required a long game. He attained at least one deuce in each of the seven games, before at last I came through. On the other hand, I was holding my serve easily, and he was never able to win more than two points from me in any service game of mine during this skein. These results bear naturally on one another, for poor Bunny was constantly under pressure. He had to work hard in an effort to hold serve, but he never was able to force *me* to work hard when I was serving. I stayed upon the attack at all times.

At last Bunny did break the vicious circle when he closed to 3-2 in the third set, but the matter was all but concluded by then. Incidentally, this was yet another finals I played in that was upset by rain, but this postponement was the least bothersome of all I encountered, for it came so extremely late in the match. We were delayed for a full half hour, but when at last Bunny and I came back on the court it took me only three minutes to conclude the action.

Bunny and I were presented to Queen Mary after the match, and she congratulated us both on our efforts. This time, I am glad to say, she neglected to make any more reference to that other match she saw us play—the one I "waved" in. Bunny himself was as gracious and warm a loser as we were friends. "I have never known such tennis as Don showed today," he told the press afterwards. I might add now in Bunny's behalf that his accomplishment of reaching the finals has grown more impressive as the years have passed, for it has turned out that his meeting with me that day remains till now the last time that an Englishman has played in his country's own men's finals.

I rounded out my last Wimbledon by sharing the men's doubles, or, as it is properly called, the four-handed championship, with Gene Mako and the mixed doubles with Alice Marble. With the same great partners helping me, I had managed to accomplish that hat trick for the first time the year before, but Bobby Riggs came right along after me and pulled the same thing off in 1939. Only Frank Sedgman (in 1952) has succeeded in winning the three titles in the same year since then.

There is even some feeling that the triple at Wimbledon is a more difficult feat than is winning the four Grand Slam singles titles. Certainly, at the time, winning the three Wimbledon championships was accorded a great deal more attention than the fact that I had now won Australia, France, and Britain and had only the United States to go for a sweep of the major tournaments in singles alone. I took off happily for the Netherlands and Czechoslovakia to play in tournaments in those countries before I headed back to the States and the Challenge Round and the last of the Grand Slam.

I arrived in Prague for the first time in my life to play in the

Czechoslovakian nationals only two months before some other gentlemen were to assemble in Munich to discuss other elements of the Czechoslovakian situation. Things were moving fast about us, as we journeyed about playing tennis that July of 1938. The Nazis were to be in Prague by the next March. The young player I beat after a long match in the first round of the Czechoslovakian championships was a local teen-age prospect whom I had never heard of named Jaroslav Drobny. It was sixteen years later, 1954, when Jaroslav Drobny, now of England, became champion of Wimbledon.

I returned to the States early in August, with Forest Hills hardly a month away. For now, though, I was forced to divert my attentions from the Grand Slam and concentrate upon the Davis Cup. The defense of the Cup was, after all, my prime goal for the year, and a defeat in it would leave the Grand Slam as a hollow achievement, even if I were able to finish it up at Forest Hills right afterwards.

The Cup matches were scheduled again for Germantown, and as they had been the year before there, the Australians were the opposition. Last year we had met the Aussies for the Interzone title. This year they had fought through to meet us in the Challenge Round. It is significant that just as Austin was the last Englishman to play in the finals of Wimbledon in 1938, the Australians were beginning an unparalleled streak of another sort. Beginning in that signal tennis year of 1938, the Aussies have not failed to make the Challenge Round since. It is coincidental to my own career, but interesting nonetheless, that in my last year as an amateur the focus of United States competition turned from Europe—from Great Britain and France—and moved to Australia, where it remains to this day.

My opening match against the Aussies found me drawing John Bromwich, whom I had last defeated back in January for the Australian crown. I felt miserable. My throat was sore and parched, and my whole body was aching with flu. The sickness had burst over me in the hours before the tie began, and in those prehistoric times before antibiotics there was no effective way that my fever could be stilled even for a while. The flu peaked on that first day against Bromwich, and I was not in my best shape.

I won the first two sets, 6-2, 6-3, much as I had overpowered him in our Australian meeting, but he came back to take the next set from me 6-4, and I barely hung on to win the match 7-5 in the fourth. Had Bromwich won that set and extended me to five sets, the edge might have become his. I was weak with flu by this time. A tooth was beginning to hurt, and I ached all over my skinny body.

Mako and I had won the National Doubles at Brookline shortly after I had returned from Europe, but now, in the second day's play, Bromwich and Quist turned on us and upset Gene and me. That was a point we had counted on, so, as it turned out, had I not held on to beat Bromwich in the first day's play, the tie would have gone to the Australians. We won only because Frankie Parker gave us a key point with a win over Adrian Quist, and then I gained the third and decisive tally with a straight-set win over Quist on the final day's play.

Somehow, 10,000 people had packed into Germantown for what was my last Davis Cup appearance, and it is ironic that while my final match was not a close contest (except for the first set, when Quist carried me to 8-6), it turned into something of a controversial imbroglio when the foot-fault arbiter, Harold Lebair, gained a certain notoriety and Quist's wrath by calling the Aussie repeatedly for foot-faults. Lebair contended that Quist was dragging his back foot (the right one) over the service line and touching it in bounds before he hit his serve.

While I was, after all, the opponent and I had a rather high degree of interest in the proceedings, I still to this day can make no judgments on the calls. I was always at the other end of the court from all that action, and, crouched down waiting for Quist to serve, I no doubt had the worst location in the house for the purpose of seeing Adrian's feet.

The defense of the Cup left me enormously elated, but I was tired, still not well, and my concern about my health returned to worry me as soon as our celebration ended. I had still felt ill playing Quist, although not as sick as I had against Bromwich two days before. The flu had begun to subside, but the pain in my tooth had developed into a ghastly full-scale toothache. What frightened me even more, though, was the fact that I was beginning to lose my voice once again. This problem was so recurrent that I could no longer pretend that it was not significant. It was now the eve of the United States championships, and though I was scared to learn the worst I knew that I had to be examined by a dentist immediately. Walter Pate recommended one in New York, and almost as soon as I checked into the Madison I reached him and he agreed to meet me in his office, even though it was late Sunday evening.

I catalogued all my recent ills to him, leading up to the toothache. I doubted that there could be any association between the loss of speech and the toothache, but I told the doctor about my repeated voice problems, and he nodded a more knowing response. When at last he peered into my mouth he seemed to quite expect what he found: a badly abscessed tooth. "Mr. Budge," he said. "The tooth has to come out immediately. I don't really understand how you've managed to get by with it for as long as you have." It was his opinion that the tooth had probably been worsening for a year or so, and that as long as eight months ago, when I was in Australia in January, it was responsible for my loss of speech. At other times throughout the year it had been acting to poison various parts of my system.

The doctor shot me full of Novocain and yanked the offending fang out right there. Although my voice continued to fail and was actually lost completely for a while, I began to feel better almost immediately, and could almost feel the poison draining out of me. As a result, Forest Hills turned out to be a much less traumatic and a much more enjoyable exercise than I could have ever expected just a few days before. Aside from the rain delay, which Gene and I turned to our most beneficial social advantage anyway, the Nationals were uneventful and almost anticlimactic.

Well, anyway, it seemed to me that they were anticlimactic, but no one quite believed me. I breezed to the finals without losing a set. Mako, unseeded, and burdened with the image of being strictly a doubles player, won his way through in the other bracket. He was the first unseeded player in fifty-seven years to make the finals, and as he went on the court to face me, this was the only fact that seemed to interest the fans. They forgot, first of all, that Mako had won his way there. A seeding is never more than a pleasant little honor and a promoter's simple device that manages to keep the luck of the draw controlled just enough so that all the supposedly best players do not happen to meet in the first round Tuesday afternoon when there is no one on hand to watch. Once a tournament begins, a seed means nothing more than yesterday's newspaper. Or: You are only as good as your last drop volley.

Also ignored was the fact that Mako *should* have been seeded in the first place. Perhaps it had already been forgotten that he had come within only two points of getting past Austin at Wimbledon in July—and Austin went on to become a finalist. Gene was playing the best singles of his life, and was probably overlooked in the seeding because he was unfairly typed as strictly a doubles player. I knew, though, that he was a much better player than some of those who had been seeded in his place. And I also knew he was hot.

To the fans, though, the fact of his being an unseeded interloper pre-empted all other consideration. Mako was to be a patsy for Budge and even a willing public sacrifice, since the two opponents were such good friends.

Oh well, this was Munich's month, and I guess myopia was catching. Gene Mako was as likely to roll over and play dead for me as peace was to come in our time. I do not recall ever sitting down with Gene and discussing the matter. There was no more need to delineate such thinking as there was for him to inscribe his intention of defeating me on our bathroom mirror with toothpaste. We both knew that our mutual compassion halted the instant that one of us threw a racket down and the other called out "rough" or "smooth." And that is the way it went in the finals.

I was a better player than Gene that day. Indeed, I usually was, for I had too much power for him. But Mako and I played together for a lot of years under all sorts of conditions, on most continents, on all surfaces, and it was unusual only when he did *not* give me a tough game. It was not an exception when he took a set from me. And this is all that happened on this occasion, for although I won the match without a great struggle, Gene made me work all the way, and he took the second set from me, 8-6. So it was that there was hardly a person on hand or anyone I have met since who does not believe that I threw that set to Gene as a token of our friendship.

The suggestion is patently ridiculous and altogether specious. First of all, whoever the opponent, such an idea was in direct opposition to my philosophy of play—keep the pressure on, never let up. Secondly, in the finals of a tournament of the stature of Forest Hills, I cannot imagine anyone taking the chance of willingly losing a set. The longer a match goes, the greater the chance of injury. In the third place, this was *this* Forest Hills, the fourth to my Grand Slam set, and under those special circumstances I would not even have *mused* on the possibility of giving up a single point to anyone, even if I were ahead 6-0, 6-0, 5-0, 40-love. Fourth, I had too much respect and affection for Gene to treat him as if he were an inferior player who could be given a set for his troubles, rather like a condescending pat on the head.

Fifth, forget all the first four logical reasons and turn to the sixth and seventh, which are founded in the same cynicism that forces the point to begin with. To be blunt, no one throws a *second* set. If you are really up to that sort of thing, you at least have the good sense to wait till the third set when you have a 2-0 lead. And no one ever throws a set at 8-6. Be sensible about it—lose a set at love or a comfortable 6-2 or 6-3, but for goodness' sake, don't wear yourself out to a frazzle playing fourteen hard games when you have no intention of winning the thing anyway.

Gene Mako beat me 8-6 in the second set of our finals. It was the only set I lost in the tournament, but I dropped it squarely. And once I had won the match, I doubt if it mattered to me one way or the other that Mako had taken a set from me. But I do know what did matter, and that is that because Gene was my last opponent, I enjoyed the warmest, most appropriate possible conclusion for my Grand Slam. When at last I hit the shot that won Forest Hills and the Grand Slam, when I rushed to the net, the man who was there to take my hand and congratulate me and smile at my triumph, was the only other man in the world who knew what I had really accomplished and how much I cared.

7

Turning Pro

For all of its early years the best tennis in the world was the amateur game. This carried through the twenties, the Tilden era, before most of the best amateurs began turning professional and giving the game's supremacy, if not always its glory, to the pros. By the time I had decided to turn pro in the late thirties there was much precedent for such a move. Several amateur champions before me had moved into the professional ranks, leaving amateur publicity and esthetics behind for one-night stands and dollars and cents.

Vinnie Richards had been the first important player to turn, in 1926, but he had not really been the top banana. That was Suzanne Lenglen, who was a bigger name as a woman than Richards as a man, for he had had to compete in the shadow of Big Bill Tilden and Little Bill Johnston. C. C. (Cash and Carry) Pyle, who also promoted such spectacles as the six-day bicycle races, was the man who signed Suzanne and Richards and gave tennis its first big pro tour.

By the time I signed, Tilden, Vines, and Perry had also all turned professional, but pro tennis then, as right up till 1968, had to struggle with talent and showmanship, but without tradition and honor. An amalgamation of the amateur and pro games, combining the strengths of both, always seemed to me to be the obvious and most natural way to present the game best. Golf, with its open format, thrived that way, but as long as the amateur tennis officials held control, they felt it best to prevent such a union. I think it hurt the game, and I think that now that the professionals have gained acceptance at last, the sport will achieve much greater popularity and prominence than ever before.

It was Wimbledon, of course, that at last welcomed the pros, and, with its great prestige, led the rest of the tennis world to do the same. I have always felt such great affection for that grand old club. To me, it was only fitting that it should be the one responsible force that at last unified the sport and gave it such a bright future.

In the summer, I conduct a tennis camp for young players at Mc-Donogh, Maryland, outside Baltimore, but in the spring of 1968, as soon as open tennis became a reality I knew immediately that whatever plans I had made, I had to arrange to be at the first open Wimbledon. I saw Jack Kramer and we decided to team up in the senior doubles. Jack said it simply and best, "Don, after all these years that we have hoped and worked for an open game, we can't let it down when finally it is a reality. We all have to be there and help it any way we can." The Grand Slam tournaments, Challenge Rounds —I doubt if there was ever any tournament that I looked forward to more than I did to the first open Wimbledon.

Well, I looked forward for thirty years. I can even remember no less a newspaper than the London *Times* speculating after my 1938 victory at Wimbledon that Fred Perry and other professionals would almost surely be permitted to challenge me for the title by the next year. Open tennis seemed so logical even then. One can only assume that tennis must be a truly exceptional game to have thrived as it has, the world over, despite such crippling from within.

Actually, I had only the finest personal association with the people who conducted amateur tennis. And indeed, in theory, amateur tennis is basically a fine idea. It's not as though it were a tricky scheme that was developed to make money, for certainly no one made much out of it. Conversely, a great deal of love and time was expended in its behalf by many people who received little tangible reward. But the ideal that amateur tennis should be preserved as the focus of the game was in dispute with the facts of the modern world. It was no more rational to ask a young man of twenty-three or twenty-five or thirty to use his special talents playing tennis for

free as it is to ask him to play baseball for free or to sell insurance
or to drive a bus for the sheer pleasure of it.

It was the rich, of course, who happened to support tennis from
its inception. It was they who cared for it, who nurtured it, who
brought it the attention and tradition it deserved as a great game. It
was also they who played it, and so there was certainly no need
for playing professionals in the early history of the game, because
the players who were most proficient were as wealthy as those who
ran the game. Despite its image as a rich man's game, though, tennis is actually a relatively inexpensive sport to play, and it became
more of a public-parks game. When the best players thus started
coming from outside of the country clubs, and the officials still remained within them, conflicts were created that were, really, never
resolved—until 1968, I think it will someday be agreed.

Big-league team sports afford opportunities for top pay to hun-
dreds of professional athletes, whereas professional tennis, an individual sport in the same sense that golf is, offers big money to only
a few. The result is that many more boys have been attracted to the
glamorous possibility of big money while wearing a Colt helmet, a
Yankee shirt, or the Celtics' satin shorts, rather than wearing their
own anonymous tennis whites with only a slim chance of making the
big time. In fact, most of the top American players of recent years
have chosen tennis primarily because their fathers were closely identified with the game. Butch Buchholz, Cliff Richey, and Marty Riessen are all sons of professionals. Dennis Ralston, Charlie Pasarell,
Clark Graebner, and Frank Froehling are sons of devoted tennis
players. Even Arthur Ashe, who might have been a star in a big-
league sport, took up tennis because his father was a caretaker for a
public court in Richmond, Virginia. But now, with the anachronistic
stand so long nourished by the tennis powers toward professionalism
giving way to open tennis (in more ways than one), and with the opportunity for a far greater number of players to make a decent living
through the game, I believe that tennis can once again begin to draw
the best young American athletes to its banner.

Ashe's dramatic victory in the first United States Open is bound
to introduce the sport to many Americans for the first time. The

great burst of interest and publicity that he received for that one victory seemed to me to exceed all the publicity that the sport has received in many years. Even before he won, though, I was pleased to see promoters and industries and television taking a new look at the game.

I only hope that tennis learns to work with its new friends rather than resist innovation. For instance, it is certainly true that the Van Alen Simplified Scoring System can make tennis better suited to television. With VASSS, scoring is patterned after ping-pong, each point counting just that: one point. Either 21 or 31 points win a set.

The obvious advantage is that a VASSS set will not run on too long. A set that goes 18-16 or something like that by conventional scoring might drag on for a couple of hours. A VASSS set that takes 31 points can be counted on to last a half hour, almost right on the button. This, of course, is perfect for TV scheduling.

Looking at the question strictly as a tennis player, I can say outright that VASSS produces an entirely different game. For instance, if you are ahead 40-love, you need only one of the next three points to win the game, and can proceed with that in mind: gamble, for instance, on an all-or-nothing shot or experiment in some way. Under the same circumstances in VASSS, you are just ahead 3-0, and since each point counts exactly the same, there is the tendency to play the next point and each succeeding one safe and the same. For an apt comparison, VASSS may be viewed as the equivalent of medal play in golf, while the conventional tennis scoring is closer to the match play ideal.

The point I am trying to make is, that even while I, and so many others in tennis, feel that VASSS is not the tennis we have known, we must be prepared to accept it if it will encourage television interest and exposure for the game. Golf, after all, hasn't done so poorly with medal play.

I turned pro because, in a competitive sense, I was forced to. Like Vines and Perry just before me and Riggs and Kramer just afterwards, I simply ran out of fields to conquer in the amateur ranks. Another factor that hurried us all to the pros was a common proclivity for eating and dressing well and putting some money in the bank. Believe me, as sure as nobody ever got rich running amateur tennis, nobody got rich playing it either. At the time I was playing as an amateur, there was nothing even approximating the situation that developed after the war, when it was often possible for a good player to make more as an amateur than as a professional.

The most I can ever remember making in expenses was $125, and we looked upon payments of such amounts as a lucky bonus and not something to be regularly expected. There was nothing very surreptitious about such deals either. Either the USLTA or the Davis Cup captain was invariably aware of them and encouraged us to accept such extra loot. Sometimes the negotiations for such exhibitions were even worked out by the tennis officials.

For example, I remember that on a couple of occasions I was invited to play in an exhibition at Detroit just after the completion of the United States Nationals. Detroit was on the way between Forest Hills and the next tournament stop in Los Angeles, so payment was a simple matter to arrange. I had my train ticket to L.A. already provided for me by tennis officials. I was given money for another one to Detroit by the people running the exhibition there—money I could pocket. That was "expenses."

Often, though, it was just three dollars a week and the buck-fifty laundry money to get by on. This stipend was paid me by my district sponsor, the Northern California Tennis Association. They also handled all my travel expenses. In return, the N.C.T.A. would receive a small part of the gate receipts from the tournaments that I entered. The U.S.L.T.A. would assume my financial obligations as soon as I began to play on the Davis Cup team in preparation for a match.

It was not high finance, and it was not very complicated. It was quite obvious to me at an early stage that no matter how good I became as an amateur, tennis was never going to make me a comfortable, self-supporting man. I had had it in my mind since my junior days to turn professional if I ever reached the top of the amateurs.

The first real pro offer I ever received came at Forest Hills in September 1937. It was from Jack Harris, the man who had promoted tours with Tilden and Vines and Vines and Perry in the previous few years. Harris's offer to me was for a $50,000 guarantee, which, particularly in terms of depression dollars, was a fair and substantial amount. It also came from a man I had known for several years and trusted.

Harris had worked for the Wilson Sporting Goods Company in Chicago, the firm whose racket I used. Harris was in charge of Wilson's golf and tennis promotion. He had moved into the tennis tour business a few years before when Ellie Vines, another Wilson representative, was touring with Tilden. Vines felt that he was being cheated at the gate, and so he called up L. B. Icely, who was then president of Wilson. Mr. Icely was a wonderful gentleman who looked after his boys, as I found out later. L. B. specified when he retired that Wilson could never sever its contract with Sam Snead or me. (As it was, I stayed with the company for two decades before I initiated the move from Wilson to the Regent Sports Company. It was an amiable parting. Wilson never reneged on Mr. Icely's stipulations.)

Anyway, when Vines called up Mr. Icely and told him he thought there was some hanky-panky going on behind his back, Mr. Icely immediately dispatched Jack Harris to go join the tour and look out for the interests of the Wilson man. Vines had not been deluding himself either. Harris casually sat in when it came time for divvying up, and sure enough, it looked as if all kinds of items were being taken off the top by Tilden's cronies before Vines's percentage was figured. Since Ellie had contracted to be paid his percentage of the gross, and since he also was establishing himself as the champ (he beat Tilden 55 matches to 22), he was apparently getting robbed. Harris stayed with the tour awhile to get the matter straightened out, and in the process he decided to get into the tour business himself.

Since Vines won the tour and since Vines was close to Harris, this was not a difficult accomplishment for Jack. After all, professional tennis operated for decades on the premise that the man who controlled the champion, controlled the game. One reason that the pros never established themselves as a viable force was that there was never any stable, coordinating professional organization to compete with the amateur organizations. Pro tennis was carried in the

hat of the man who had the best player under contract, and sometimes, in the case of first Bobby Riggs and then Jack Kramer, the
organization was simplified even more since promoter and champion
wore the same fedora.

Anyway, Harris was the man with the tour at that time. He was
young and clever and a real friend of mine, so I could not help but
be pleased—and tempted—when he made the offer. I had already
made up my mind, however, that I should stay an amateur for one
more year and defend the Davis Cup at home. This extra time
would give the United States a greater opportunity to develop a
player who could then be prepared to step right in and take my
place as team leader.

I explained this to Harris, and he accepted my decision with understanding. He did not pressure me any further except to make one
point. "Don," he said. "I can't argue with you, but I do want you to
be aware of one thing. A year of tennis is a lot of matches and a lot
of quick stops and a lot of falls. It could happen, you know. You
could turn a knee or rip a muscle one day in the third round of some
tournament that doesn't mean a blasted thing, and that'll be it.
You'll be through as a player with nothing to show for it except the
silverware. You've thought of that?"

I had. Often. "Oh, I know that, Jack," I said. "I've weighed that
possibility, I understand it, and I've just decided that the gamble is a
good one. Besides," I added, referring somewhat mysteriously to
the Grand Slam that I had already begun to plot, "if I do what I
want to do with thirty-eight, Jack, it's going to cost you a lot more
money next year."

Harris may have been a little mystified by my curious reference,
but he took it smiling. "Okay, Don," he said. "I hope I see you this
time next year, and I hope you're worth more money to both of us."

In the Grand Slam year that followed, speculation began to grow,
of course, that I would turn pro at the end of the year. I tried to
avoid the question, for I really did not want to think about the matter seriously until I had to. Of course, that was hardly possible, but
the less said about the potential signing, the easier it was for me. I
was surprised in one sense, though, for I had anticipated a repetition

of appeals to my staying amateur on the basis of patriotism. That had been a theme often voiced when a top amateur wanted to desert the Davis Cup team and sign. However, I was spared all but a trace of such talk. Apparently, people were beginning to understand that tennis pros were not really much different from what they had been as amateurs except that they had developed the faculty of being able to pick up checks, just like others gainfully employed.

Still, however, there did remain a stigma attached to the tennis professional. A few people, with the best of intentions, warned me seriously that as a pro I would forfeit the chance to go into a country club through the front door. Even had this been the case—and, on the contrary, I have never once been refused use of a country-club front door—the reasoning is far wide of the mark. I can assure you that however much self-respect one feels going through a front door, he feels a great deal more pride in being able to pay his way which-ever door he may go through.

The few small, nagging doubts I had about turning pro were com-pletely erased from my mind by Little Bill Johnston, the man who ranked just below Tilden for much of the twenties. Bill had never turned professional, so I imagined that he had very good reasons for staying an amateur and would serve as a perfect devil's advocate for me. To my surprise, though, Johnston turned out to be more ve-hemently in favor of my signing than anyone else I had talked to.

"Take it, Don," he said, hardly pausing to consider my question. "I was offered thirty-to-forty thousand to sign a few years ago, and I thought I would. Then a lot of people started telling me not to. They gave me that line about having to go in the back doors. They told me the country needed me to play tennis for the Davis Cup. I was just plain un-American if I turned pro. So I thought about it, Don, and everybody seemed so certain that at last it got to me and I turned the offer down. Well, you know what happened. A year or so later I came down with TB. I needed money then, but I couldn't get my hands on it. All those friends who had urged me to stay ama-teur for the sake of Uncle Sam turned their backs on me as soon as I needed them. Take the money, Don," Bill told me. "The pats on the back don't last very long at all."

I took it, and I took all I could get. I met with Jack Harris once again before the '38 Forest Hills, and this time I told him I was ready to sign after the Nationals if the price was right. "I offered you fifty thousand dollars last year," Jack said. "I'll make it sixty now." I told Jack that wasn't the right price.

"Look, Jack," I said, "I think you know I'm not a hard man. I'm not out to rob you. But this is the one time in my life when I am in the driver's seat. If I don't get what I want from you, Jack—and I do want to sign with you—I'm pretty sure I can look around and get it somewhere else."

"What do you want?"

"Seventy-five," I said. He started to talk. "But wait a minute, Jack. I want the seventy-five thousand as a guarantee, but I also want to put that up against a percentage that we can work out. If we draw more people than we think we can right now, I want to share in the extra."

Harris was generally agreeable, and after Forest Hills we went into detailed negotiations in earnest. The fact that I won and moved back into the headlines did not hurt my position. I was also honored to have Walter Pate, who was not only a highly respected lawyer but the very pillar of amateur tennis, serve as my counsel. He drew up the basic contract for me, worked out the details with Harris, and advised me in all legal matters. If there had been any temptation on the part of the amateur establishment to criticize my decision, I am sure that the role that Pate played stilled such talk before it even began. Similarly, none of the top tennis writers condemned me either. Fellows like Allison Danzig of the *Times,* Al Laney of the *Herald Tribune,* and Jim Burchard of the *World-Telegram* all supported my decision, and none even suggested that I was any less a patriot for it.

I signed with Harris officially on December 20, 1938, in Walter Pate's Manhattan law office. Harris had agreed on the $75,000 guarantee against percentage, and we got the full play of the newspapers and newsreels and radio. A few days before Christmas, sports editors were having trouble filling up all their space with baseball Hot Stove League scoops. While the cameras whirled, I inked my pact, as they say, and Harris presented me with a certified check for $25,000. The arrangement was fixed so that I would receive a second $25,000 installment in March, 1939, and the third and final $25,000 early in 1940. That way I could spread the one-year tour contract over three calendar years and get the most advantageous tax break. I really do not like to belabor talk of money, but, in retrospect, the most interesting aspect of the whole deal was that my total tax bill for the three years came to about $5200. Bring back the thirties! I should point out too that the tour succeeded beyond our fondest hopes, and I ended up making more than $100,000. It is possible—I do not know for sure—that I was the only athlete to make six figures except for heavyweight boxers until DiMaggio did a decade later.

One of the major reasons why we made so much more money than had been anticipated was that Harris had worked out a new tour format. In previous years when a new amateur champion broke in to challenge the top pro, the tour was booked into every town in the forty-eight states with a room or corridor large enough to hold a tennis court. Pro tennis would throw down its canvas and start to play in the middle of a street if a few stragglers had gathered to watch the aftermath of an automobile accident. Vines and Perry had played that kind of tour, winding on a serpentine route that carried them into just about every county seat in the nation. They probably would have hit even more spots, but in the winter we were restricted almost always to playing indoors. We did play a few matches outside in the more southern areas, but invariably we were inside. Abroad, in the summer, we were mostly scheduled out of doors. The indoor tennis vaudeville circuit was an American phenomenon.

The Vines-Perry tour had ended up pretty evenly, though, so while Vines had held a slight edge and kept his world title, Fred had hardly been disgraced, and could not be counted out of any future competition for the championship. There was also still an obvious market for Perry-Budge matches; after all, I had never yet beaten Fred in an important confrontation. Therefore, Harris hit on the idea of back-to-back tours. Instead of playing all the tank towns, we would hit the bigger cities twice. The first time around I would play Vines. That, after all, was the hotter attraction. But then, after our tour finished, I would come back on a similar circuit against Fred, assuming I beat Vines. We didn't figure to draw as well the second time around, but we did figure—and the assumption was correct—that we could draw better a second time in the larger cities than just once in the watering holes.

It was a good plan, the first primitive sophistication of tennis barnstorming, and it made us all more money. As expected, though, Ellie and I were a much greater attraction than Fred and I were to be. Vines and I opened in Madison Square Garden just two weeks after I signed the contract, on January 2, 1939. We drew a standing room crowd of 17,000, and tickets were scaled as high as $7.70. That was a fantastic price to pay in those days, but the scalpers were getting three times that out on Eighth Avenue. The total gate was $47,120—and they sold some hot dogs and beer too—and with such obvious interest the effect was such as to almost assure the whole tour success by the time we got to the next stop, Boston.

I beat Ellie that first night 6-3, 6-4, 6-2, creating the misconception that I was to roll over Vines on the tour. I did edge him out by a match score of 22-17, but it was the exception when our matches were not close. I took a 2-0 lead by winning in Boston, but then he came right back with victories in Philadelphia and Chicago and returned things to their proper perspective. We played those opening four matches the best of five sets, but the balance of the tour was contested two-out-of-three sets. Two other pros, Al Chapin and Bruce Barnes, also traveled with us. They would play the preliminary match and then after Ellie and I went in the feature, we would pair up with Chapin and Barnes and face each other in the doubles as well. That was the way a typical tour schedule went in those days.

We never traveled by plane, but usually used trains when we were playing in the East, and switched to cars—station wagons, really—when we moved into the West. Harris had worked out some sort of promotional deal, and we would get a couple of the station wagons on loan to carry us. There were also two maintenance men who were part of the troupe. They had their own truck, which was our circus wagon. On the side it had something emblazoned like "PROFESSIONAL TENNIS CHAMPIONSHIP OF THE WORLD. Ellsworth Vines vs. Don Budge" with bright colors and other effects.

The two fellows who ran the truck were amazing. They never missed a city, and many times we played back-to-back nights in places fairly far apart. There were times when they got bogged down in snow—we were usually playing in the wintertime—or suffered flat tires or run-down batteries, but like the mail, they always got the canvas through on time.

Actually, the only reason we needed two maintenance men was that so many of the distances were so great that one man could not drive the full route. With two men, one could curl up and sleep while the other put on the miles. The truck would leave immediately after we had finished the doubles match. At first, we usually operated our own schedule with morning departures, but after awhile we began to move like the truck—at night, right after the matches.

After a hard match, it is impossible to get to sleep for hours anyway, so it made more sense to travel at night instead of tossing and turning and then getting up at the crack of dawn and moving when we *were* sleepy. Most of the professional teams try to travel this way now. It is fitting the round peg in the round hole. Most of the players I have traveled with soon developed the capacity of being able to catnap in the most interesting places, but I never traveled with a player who could fall asleep right after a tough match. You are just too keyed up.

When we could, then, we would leave right after a match and drive as far as possible that night, stopping only when we were all just too tired to continue. Often we would just pull in at random into some tourist cabins or a small-town hotel. More than once we startled some wizened old room clerk, who would be slumped down, half asleep, when we would barge in at two or three in the morning. And here we would come, five strange young men, beards heavy and voices gruff, grumbling at the hour and the hotel, piling out of two mud-splattered station wagons. No one in his right mind would take us for tennis players. We were obviously highwaymen.

The following morning we could sleep late and still make the next town in time—Cincinnati, Louisville, Indianapolis, Fort Wayne, and so on. Our advance publicity man had preceded us by a couple of weeks, so by the time we arrived interviews and store appearances usually had already been arranged. Invariably, at each stop there was at least one cynical old sports editor also waiting, ready to scoop the world and let everybody in on the fact that the whole tour was a fix, and that both Ellie and I were in cahoots in trying to keep the score close.

Ellie and I would patiently try to explain that there was just too much money on the line (not to mention the prestige) for the future for whoever carried the title, but our disclaimers never seemed to satisfy the skeptics we met at each stop. For one thing, I was already pegged as the guy who had thrown a set to my buddy at Forest Hills, so there was no reason why I should not also be chucking them to Vines to keep things exciting. On February 6, 1939, I had one of those nights when I could do no wrong. We were in New Orleans, playing before a good crowd, and I beat him 6-0, 6-1. That is bad enough, but to make it worse, the whole massacre took only fifteen minutes.

Jack Harris was frantic. He came out on the court and spoke to us. "Play another set," he said. "Let's make it three out of five." Ellie just shook his head, and then he looked at his watch. "Jack," he said, "there's no use in that. The way Don is playing that would just be another seven and a half minutes. Come on, let's start the doubles." For the cynics who had their minds made up about the tour, though, I guess that even this performance could not change the opinion that Ellie and I must be playing only to keep it close and exciting for the fans.

I needed no special incentive to play Ellie either. It may be difficult to imagine how I could get up every night to play the same guy, but considering what was riding on every match—the world championship—I never had any trouble preparing myself to play Vines. The fact that he had been my idol for years was another factor that made me want to beat him all the more. It was like eating when you were hungry, and the fact that he and I were playing the same

opponent every night made no difference at all in my mental out-
look. I was ready every night.

The tour was not a grueling life, if only because I was young
and it was all new and exciting. It was, however, a strenuous day-
to-day existence, and we were both pushed to our physical limits from
the start. I can remember coming into Pittsburgh, which was only
the fifth stop on the whole tour. Ellie and I had split the first four
matches, and this time, in the Duquesne Gardens, we went right to
the wire before I won the third and deciding set at 11-9. We staggered to the locker room, changed into some dry clothes, and went
right back out for the doubles. That was a long, tough match too,
and when at last we got back to the locker room, my feet were in
agony.

I pulled off my shoes as gingerly as I could. The bottoms of my
feet were covered with blood that was gushing from several big
broken blisters. "Ellie," I said, "how in the world am I going to keep
playing this tour? We've hardly started and look at my feet already."

Ellie only chuckled. "Well kid," he said, "take a look at these."
He carefully pulled a shoe and the sock off of one of his feet, and, if
possible, the sight revealed was even uglier and bloodier than the
one my feet had presented.

Because we were playing the bigger cities, which generally have
the better arenas, the conditions were not as bad as might have been
expected. The canvas we played on, which was usually stretched
over a basketball court, was a fast surface, about the speed of grass,
but it was smooth and fair. The bounces were always true. Besides,
both Ellie and I had good eyes, so it was seldom that the bad lighting bothered us.

Dim lighting certainly does affect an indoor game, but like the
weather, it operates in equal measure upon both players. The most
distracting aspect of the indoor lighting was that the various light fix-
tures themselves were located in a different pattern in the ceiling of
each auditorium. You never could be sure how to prepare your eyes
when you looked up to hit an overhead, because you never knew exactly where the glare would be coming from. Most of us accepted
that fact as a disconcerting element that was unfortunate but was not

worth the added irritation of worrying about it. Tilden, however, was always on edge about the lights. As soon as he hit a new town, he would hurry out to the arena, and find some electrician or maintenance man and start directing him all over the roof, having him fuss with the angle of this light, tilting that one the other way. Tilden would stand down on the floor where the canvas would be laid, and go through the motion of hitting overheads. Then he would send the poor electrician scurrying back and forth across the ceiling, adjusting a light so that it no longer glared directly in Tilden's eyes as he hit the imaginary overhead. It was our joke that Tilden required so many changes that the lighting arrangement ended up exactly as it had been before he started fussing with it.

Hitting an overhead either indoors or out in the bright sun is always difficult anyway, because the ball is dropping so fast that any player must develop sharp coordination between eye and arm to pull off a good shot. An overhead is essentially like a serve and should be hit as one serves (and, again, as one throws a pitch), except that the ball is coming down too quickly for one to have the chance to wind-up for an overhead.

Remember, on the serve, you take the racket down by the side of your leg as you prepare to hit, then swing it up on a great circle route before you at last cock your elbow and make the hit. You can't use all this motion before you hit an overhead. The ball is dropping too fast.

For the overhead, you must concentrate first on making contact. When you see a lob go up, move to the spot where the ball should drop, while pointing your racket at the ball, cradling the racket throat in your left hand, so that you are affecting the position of a bird shooter with a shotgun. Get the ball clearly in your sights.

At last, as the ball makes the final drop, cock your elbow quickly, draw your racket back behind you, so that your hand is by your ear, and then, with just that half-swing, punch the ball home. In the overhead, remember the simple sequence: point, cock, half-swing. The less elaborate your effort, the more success you will consistently have. The player who manages to hit a big booming roundhouse of an overhead may impress the crowd occasionally with one of those crushing smashes that bounces over the fence and into kingdom come, but more often he will hit the ball out or even miss it altogether. Henri Cochet of France could never be trapped into trying a big smash, but he had a consistently good overhead. It was not powerful at all—indeed, Cochet had a poor serve—but he had complete control of his overhead, and did not need great power. If necessary, he would angle off two or three successive soft overheads before he finally would be able to put one away.

The hardest part in hitting the overhead probably comes after you have hit it. The natural tendency is to begin to follow the ball with your eye as soon as you have hit it. Don't. Concentrate on keeping your eye on the spot where you have made contact with the ball, and keep your eye there until after you have followed through. It is the same principle that is so often heard about keeping your eye on the golf tee until after you have completed the swing. There is a natural anxiety to look away, following the ball, but if you do, you will hit a bad tee shot as sure as a bad overhead. It is hard enough to hit a rapidly falling ball solidly in the middle of your racket without looking away at what you think is the moment of contact. Too often you will look up before you actually hit, or you will jump as you hit and not follow through easily.

A great case can be made for the claim that the overhead is the most difficult shot to hit in tennis. Whether that is true or not is moot; it is hard enough, and many great players were forever baffled by it. Tilden, for instance, had the great cannonball serve, but he could never hit an authoritative overhead (whether he had the lights arranged properly or not). Bill had to angle his overheads off and steer them softly to achieve what small success he had.

Often he let a lob bounce first before hitting it back, and you may want to consider doing this if the overhead continues to frustrate you. Letting the lob hit the ground takes you farther back from the net and reduces your hitting angle, but hitting the ball on the bounce is unquestionably an easier thing to do. After a good bounce, a ball tends to sit up there, lazier and fatter.

In some cases, especially when you just do not have the time to get set and aim, it is best to be prudent, let the ball bounce, and take the safer overhead farther back. The one player I can remember who virtually *never* hit an overhead off the bounce was Ted Schroeder, the 1949 Wimbledon champion and a great Davis Cup player. I would not advise you to be quite as determined as Ted was to hit an overhead without a bounce under all circumstances, but I would suggest that you give the shot a full test. Then, if it still fazes you too much, let the lob bounce before you try to hit it.

In my own case, I always tried to hit the ball without a bounce whenever possible. However, if I felt that the lob had gone too high and was coming down too fast, or if I found that staring up at the ball was sort of mesmerizing me (that happens a lot more than you might imagine), why then I would back up, shake the glare from my eyes and play an overhead off the bounce.

Whether you are moving up or back to get under an overhead, your movement should always be made by first turning your body sideways to the net, and then skipping that way, sideways, up or back. You are looking up, remember, pointing the racket, concentrating on making contact with the ball, so if you are crossing your feet as you move you are quite likely to get tangled up. The same principles apply in such sports as football and basketball, where the man on defense tries to make his moves without crossing one leg over the other.

The overhead is much like the serve, so it is not surprising that players who serve well also hit good overheads. Tilden was the exception to this rule, but the good servers who did also develop good overheads all had to learn that the service motion cannot be fully duplicated for use in hitting an overhead. You must shorten the swing on the overhead. The players who hit both shots well all followed that maxim. Some of the best I have seen were: Jaroslav Drobny, maybe the best left-handed overhead hitter; Kramer, who often played doubles with Schroeder; Gonzales, whom I would rate as just below Kramer with this shot; and Vines, whom I would rank just above Jack as the best of all, just as I list him tops with the serve too.

Of course, it has always been difficult for me to be objective about Ellie's talents. Before I met him he was my idol; afterwards, he was always my close friend. We had known each other for several years before I finally played him in '39, but I looked forward to meeting Vines on that tour with as much trepidation as excitement. He had been at the top of the tennis world for almost a decade by then, and he had so dominated the game that his interest in tennis had begun to wander and he had begun to be intrigued by golf. In fact, by the time I turned pro, Vines had already decided that he would turn his full efforts to golf as soon as he lost the world championship of tennis.

If Ellie was looking ahead to other horizons, however, I do not believe that he was yet failing in tennis. He was, after all, still beating all comers, just as he had been doing for years. He was not old either, though there was that deceptive thought sometimes if only because he had been so precocious. Ellie had first won the Nationals in 1931 when he was all of nineteen. He was still only a very lively twenty-six when I turned pro and was first able to play him.

Still, if I had not let Ellie know that I eventually wanted to become a professional, he might have deserted tennis for golf even earlier than he actually did. We had long been close friends and practice competitors, and Vines wanted to have a real go against me before he pulled out of the game.

Vines was always good company, quiet and more reliable, say, than he was on the court, where he sometimes tended to extremes. (That was perhaps his greatest tennis weakness.) He had a slow drawl that was somewhat deceptive, for he possessed a deep reservoir of solid good sense and the kind of sure temperament that is usually associated with a well-clipped resonant baritone. He was not the sort who provoked all sorts of funny little incidental recollections. What I do recall of Ellie are numerous occasions, all blended together now, when we were all together on tour and trying to decide something. We would all discuss the various possibilities and offer our suggestions while Vines would sit by and listen.

Finally, someone would remember to ask the quiet man, and Vines would say something like, "Well, I've just been listening to all the things you had to say, and well, maybe we ought to do it this way." And sure enough, that was invariably the simplest and best way. Ellie had great perspective, and he never deluded himself. When he did announce his retirement, Allison Danzig kidded with him and told him it was too soon to retire. Allison asked him why he didn't play for a few more years.

"Look," Ellie said, "tennis used to be an awful lot of fun for me. I'd stand in one place and hit the ball from one side to another and watch the other guy chase it back and forth until finally he couldn't catch up with it, and I'd win the point. It was a marvelous game, and I loved it. Now, unfortunately, about halfway through the tour with Budge, it occurred to me that something wasn't quite the same. I thought about it, and one time, when I was standing there between points trying to get my breath, I realized that what was different was that all of a sudden I was the other guy. He was standing in one spot, and I was the one doing all the running back and forth. That's when I made up my mind that it was time to retire." If this was true, how come I lost about five pounds every match?

Ellie was a little more specific with me after the tour. "Don," he said, "it was that damn backhand of yours down the line that broke my back."

I told Vines that I wished he had let me in on that a little earlier. It would have made me feel a great deal more confident. In the end, though, I did beat him, and I also beat Perry in the bargain, for when I started tangling with Fred after my tour with Vines closed, I had little difficulty with the man I had never won a big match from in the amateurs.

It was simply that after enduring Vines's power game, I never felt any real pressure when playing Fred. I opened against him on March 10, 1939, in Madison Square Garden, but this opening drew only 7000 and an appropriately smaller gate as well. I whipped Perry 6-1, 6-3, 6-0 in forty-nine minutes, and that rout removed a lot of drama from the tour from the first. The score in matches ended up 28-8 in my favor, so that by the summer of '39 I had clearly established myself as the world champion.

Unfortunately, the world that was still safe for tennis (or cared about it) was shrinking fast when Vines, on his swansong, Lester Stoefen, Tilden, and myself took off after the Perry tour to play some exhibitions and tournaments in Europe, Africa, Asia, and Australia. We were booked around the world into 1940. Harris was having no trouble at all finding dates for us. The balance of power and the interest had, for the moment, definitely switched to professional tennis, and we were in demand.

There is no doubt that the war came just as my game crested. What more I might have accomplished had there been no war is a natural speculation, but, really, an idle one. Maybe Bob Feller would have won thirty games in one season if there had been no war; maybe Tom Dewey would have been elected President.

At the time of the war, the United States had definitely assumed command as the dominant tennis power in the world. We are a pro-oriented country when it comes to athletics, and at that time, our best players were either already professional or on the verge of turning. Had there been no war to stop what seemed a natural momentum toward accepting the pros, I think it is quite likely that open tennis would have arrived nearly three decades before at last it did.

Our tour ended in London in September of 1939. Some dates were canceled; other engagements we simply could not get to. The cost to me alone was at least $40,000 in guarantees, and, with luck, I might have earned twice that had we been able to go on. None of us really wanted to go back to the States, because we felt the war scare would be neatly cleared up in six months, so we could come back in the spring and pick up exactly where we left off.

Indeed, until at last we made the final decision to go home, there was great sentiment among us to take a British ship, the *Arundel Castle,* to Egypt, where we were already booked. Had we been able to receive any assurance at all that the ship would be escorted, we most surely would have taken her. There was no definite word forthcoming from any source, however, until at last Jack Harris got through to someone at the Admiralty. When even they could not guarantee that the *Castle* would be escorted to Egypt, we decided to go back to the States.

We took an American ship to New York. It was a liner carefully marked with United States flags painted all over it, a fact we noted at first somewhat blithely. We were not so smug for long, though, for a couple of days out from Southampton the word came that the *Arundel Castle* had been sunk with great loss of life en route to Egypt. It was not really until then that we understood that we were not likely to be back in London in the spring to play tennis. For the first time, in fact, we appreciated how one could be grateful just to be alive.

The war in Europe and the lack of original, strong opposition combined to keep me more or less on the sidelines in the year that followed. I moved to New York and did promotional work. It was the first time in almost a decade that I had really been away from the game, and the feeling was naturally peculiar. The next year, 1941, came, and I was still dressed up with no place to go. Vines was in golf by now; I had spoiled any further market for matches with Perry by beating him so decisively in '38; and no amateurs were ready to sign up to challenge me.

At last, then, Jack Harris arranged for me to tour against Tilden head-to-head. Big Bill was forty-eight by then, so the draw for the main bout would be mostly curiosity and sentimentality, but we figured it was better than staying in New York. After all, Tilden had been past his prime for a decade now, but he still managed to remain a popular gate attraction.

He was still capable of some sustained great play that could occasionally even carry him all the way through a match. Most of the time he could, at his best, hang on for at least a set or two. Despite his age, he was no pushover. His years were somewhat deceptive anyway. For instance, just a couple of years before, Bill had taken a medical test in order to obtain a policy from the Prudential Life Insurance Company. Those who studied the tests sent them back with the notation that there had been some mistake in listing the subject's age. He could not be in his mid-forties, for the tests indicated that this man applying for insurance had the heart and lungs of a man twenty-five years old. Tilden was a most formidable forty-eight.

The people, of course, came out primarily for the show—to see me at my peak, and to see Tilden because they might never have the chance again. On that basis it really was a valid evening's entertainment because, as I indicated, Bill could invariably manage to keep things close for awhile. It was seldom, however, that he could extend me to the end, and I swamped him on the whole tour, fifty-five matches to six.

The next year should have brought the inception of a valid pro tennis competition. Late in 1941 Bobby Riggs turned pro and so did Frankie Kovacs. Together with Perry and myself we were formed into a round robin that provided regular but varied competition and a new level in pro tennis. Lex Thompson was now handling the promotion, and even though the war in Europe was still shadowing us all, it appeared as though we could at last begin to move pro tennis out of a barnstorming era and closer to the big time. We were negotiating the last of the big arena contracts and were preparing to kick things off with a big publicity blast for the press on the day that the Japanese bombed Pearl Harbor.

We managed to go through a tour, but it could not be anywhere near as comprehensive as originally planned, and everyone's mind was somewhere else. I did win the tour, finishing ahead (in order) of Riggs, Perry, and Kovacs, but the triumph was hollow and brief. Not long after we finished, I was off to the Army Air Corps. I earned a commission and became a tactical officer assigned to special services. I never coached tennis but instead worked in operating various physical conditioning programs.

Unfortunately, a certain lack of conditioning was to cost me a great deal. While I was waiting for an opening in an OCS class, I was assigned to the base in Wichita Falls, Texas. One cold day there, in the best of service tradition, our whole company was standing around, waiting. We happened to be lined up next to an obstacle course that we were scheduled to contend with later, but an energetic sergeant thought we could best serve ourselves by using the idle time to practice on the course. Where we were waiting was, however, not at the beginning of the course, but about mid-way in it, where the obstacles were of a more difficult nature. The particular hurdle that first confronted me was a high fence. I was to climb it, grab a rope near the top and then swing over it and move on to the next test.

In the normal course of the exercise, it was not a tremendously difficult feat, but without any warm-up I should not have tried it. I reached up for the rope, and while I was struggling to lift myself over, I tore a muscle in my shoulder. The pain was excruciating right away. I even took twenty c.c.s of Novocain, but without notable success. The tear didn't heal, and the scar tissue that was formed complicated the injury and made it even more serious.

Nevertheless, though the injury was painful and damaging, it healed enough so that I was able to carry on with my military duties. The pain was irregular. It would disappear altogether for awhile and then suddenly come back, for instance, when I was drying off and reached behind myself to towel off my back. The injury stayed with me that way, nagging, menacing, and as long as two years afterwards, in the spring of '45, I was given a full month's medical leave so that I could go to Berkeley and have an osteopath, Dr. J. LeRoy Near, work with me.

With that help and the natural healing processes, the shoulder had improved enough so that later in that summer I played quite a bit of tennis in the Pacific in a series of Army-Navy Davis-Cup-style matches. I teamed with Frank Parker, who had finally won the Nationals the year before as Sergeant Frank Parker. (He repeated in 1945.) Bobby Riggs and Wayne Sabin represented the Navy. Parker, the amateur, thus earned the distinction of playing in an open tennis match while United States amateur champion. Of course, it took a world war to bring about such an event.

We played these matches for the entertainment of servicemen in stops from Honolulu west to the Mariana Islands. We even played one match on Tinian Island at just about the time that planes were lifting off from the Tinian airstrip, carrying the A-bombs to Hiroshima and Nagasaki. That was about as close as I came to combat. Frankie and I also lost the series 3-2, and shortly thereafter I was separated from the service because the war was over. Riggs and I had already begun making plans for a tour.

Almost as soon as all the arrangements had been completed, I began to realize that my serve was not what it had been. The shoulder no longer bothered me, but I had compensated for the injury for so long, holding my elbow in tight to my body as I served, that that had become natural for me, and I could not get my old swing back. I should have postponed the tour till I was back in form. After all, *I* had the championship. But after all the war years I was naturally eager to get going again, and I was positive I could win anyway. Besides, all the plans had been made, and everybody realized that the postwar boom was on. People wanted to get out and enjoy themselves again. Just open up the gates and we had to make money.

Everything went right except my serve, and, for the same reason, my overhead. Bobby was a great lobber, and he kept throwing them up and I kept missing with my overheads. Riggs took the first twelve matches from me and then led 13-1 before I was finally able to establish enough of a new style to give him a fight. But the tour was not quite long enough for me, and I was never able to catch him.

The tour had been billed as a natural contest of styles between the slugger (me) and the clever boxer (Riggs). As such, it would have been the classic battle. Unfortunately, it never worked out that way. I could never get the swing to serve with the power I had owned. In the end I was really trying to outsteady Bobby. I was just trying to beat him at his own game. The adjustment I made was difficult and necessary, but it was not an entirely new style I switched to. After all, I grew up playing as the steady little retriever, and it was just a case of going back in time a dozen or so years. I almost caught Riggs, too. I came back at him from the 13-1 deficit to finish behind only 24-22. So it was, that in my last days as champion I won twenty-one and lost eleven matches but lost the title.

After the tour I visited with George Toley, who is still the pro at the Los Angeles Tennis Club and the coach of the team at the University of Southern California that always wins or is a contender for the national collegiate title. George is one of the finest teaching pros in the country—some of his later stars at USC were to be Alex Olmedo, Dennis Ralston, Rafael Osuna, Stan Smith, and Bob Lutz —and it took him about five minutes to steer me back on the right track. "Look, Don," George said. "You're half hitting the serve and half pushing it. You've gone so far off, you're doing so many things wrong, that it is too late to try to correct it. Don, to get your serve back, we're going to have to make you start learning it all over again from scratch."

That is what we did, too. One particularly helpful aid we employed was motion pictures. It was the first time I had ever used them to good advantage. First, we would look at the old pictures of myself serving, when I had the groove. Then we would compare them with pictures that had just been developed, showing my present form. The juxtaposition of the two right before my eyes was a startling shock. I had had no idea how much I had changed my style until George let me see the difference.

Nevertheless, the help came too late. By the time I got my serve back, my legs had started to go. This was especially true since I could not get the steady competition that I needed. After Riggs beat me, he overlooked me the next time and took Kramer, the big new name, on tour against him. It was too bad for me, but I don't blame Bobby now, and I didn't then. It was not his fault, but the system's. If I had been, say, a golfer under similar circumstances, I think I could have played my way back into shape on the tour. In pro tennis, however, the only accepted game was a head-to-head confrontation, and no one else had anywhere to go.

Still, I came close to an effective comeback under the opportunities available to me. In 1946, when I was still struggling with my serve, Riggs beat me in the finals of the United States Professional Championships at Forest Hills in three quick and easy sets. By the next year, though, I was able to carry him to five sets in the finals, and in the '48 championships I had Jack Kramer down 2-1 in sets and with two service breaks in the fourth set in the semis before I crumpled with cramps and he went on to win easily. I was thirty-three then, not yet ancient for the game, but I was lacking in competition. I think that was a much greater factor in my loss than my age itself.

If I had won then I would have been right back in the heat of things too, but the defeat left me nowhere, for Jack, who had succeeded Riggs by then as tour head as well as champion, was looking for fresh, young names, and such players as Gonzales and Sedgman were the more natural attractions. Another sad fact about tennis before it became an open game is that it not only legislated against good athletes who might enter the sport, but it also made it difficult for the good ones to remain in it.

8

Doubles—the Older You Get . . .

The older you get, the more your tennis is going to be doubles, and this is true whether you are a duffer or world class.
Doubles provides a rejuvenation of interest in the sport, a new life at forty, and it also requires a lot of people to take a new look at tennis. Many can play singles for years and hardly ever come up over the baseline—just get the ball in play and get it back and manage a very reliable game with ground strokes and little else. If you are going to play doubles, though, you are really going to have to learn more about the requirements of the net game because in doubles it is at the net where the points are won and lost.

Of course, the net game is hardly just something for doubles. At the higher levels of competence in today's serve-and-rush play, net is a vital part of singles. No one could last long at all in today's competition without a reliable net game. Without one, you would be swamped.

That is why I say, incidentally, that Bill Tilden simply cannot be rated anywhere near the top in any listing of the best players in the history of tennis. Surely Bill dominated his era as perhaps no one else ever has. But also, Bill was lucky that his time was the Roaring Twenties, a decade that has certainly had the best press agentry of any in civilized history. The stars of the twenties all ended up larger than life, and the one best in every sport profited by association with famous counterparts in other sports. Thus, while Tilden, Bobby

Jones, Babe Ruth, Red Grange, and even Man o' War may have unquestionably been the best in their sport at that time, they have all been lumped together in glory so often that it is almost impossible to suggest that one may *not* be the greatest ever without seeming to demean the whole group.

I certainly do not want to put down any one of the greats of the twenties or any cherished memories, but I still maintain that however outstanding Bill was for his time, any number of players who followed him would be too good for him, for they could exploit his net deficiencies terribly. I would suggest that Vines, Kramer, Gonzales, Laver, Rosewall, Sedgman, Segura, Perry, Cramm, and Riggs have been the best of all, and that Tilden would rank below those players, probably around twelfth or so.

Tilden did, of course, possess many great attributes; it is just that all those I rank above him would have quickly learned to get into the net after his weak second serve and dominate play from there. The reverse would also apply when Tilden was receiving serve, for he knew that he did not have a good net game, and he was bashful about moving to the net when he had a good chance to attack. Bill simply did not have the all-court game that quite a few players since him have possessed.

Tilden also had little competition, so his big serve could intimidate many of his challengers. A player like Henri Cochet, who gave Tilden fits and regularly beat him, owned a serve that could not break an egg. Cochet's sweeping shovel backhand was a great deal more artistic than it was hard. I've seen movies of Cochet and other opponents playing Big Bill, and Tilden has an incredible amount of time in each case in which to dance around in the backcourt and get into position before the shot is returned. Off Cochet's little serve, Tilden should have followed his big return to the net on each occasion, but he lacked the net game and stayed back, and too often Cochet would eventually pitty-pat Big Bill into submission.

Tilden's time was a great one for tennis, though, and I am not going to stand on a soap box and wave a flag and suggest that my era must have been the very best. I do think that the prewar decade produced an exceptional number of outstanding players, but we did not produce anywhere near the vast number of good and very good players that are now on the scene.

It was rare in our time that the top seeds had any serious threat until they were well along into a tournament, even a Wimbledon or a Forest Hills. Today's best amateurs must contend with fine opponents from the very first round on. Nothing pointed that up more than in the 1967 Wimbledon when Manuel Santana, first-seeded and defending champion, was upset in the first round by Charlie Pasarell, who was not considered good enough to play for a losing United States Davis Cup team. Ecuador would not even have bothered to play us in my time, much less beat us, as they did in 1967. It is inconceivable that anything like that could have happened in the thirties.

One major reason that the fields are so much deeper now is that tennis has so much greater scope. Countries that seldom produced a player of any substance in my day are now capable of fielding strong Davis Cup squads. Kids are getting the best international competition when they are still only fifteen or sixteen. There are more courts everywhere, there are more opportunities, and there are just more good players. I am sure without a doubt that playing in today's tournaments would be more difficult for me than it was in the thirties. In those days I could suffer a bad match in an early round and still manage to pull it out. Today, I would be pressed throughout.

Of course, to be crotchety, today's players have advantages that my generation would certainly not have minded suffering. The thing that came closest to causing me to lose one of my Grand Slam tournaments was one of my various mysterious ailments. Today, I would have been diagnosed between sets, shot full of penicillin, and sent back out again, well. Or to be even more prosaic, consider the matter of my long white gabardines, which have become something of a trade-mark for me, since I wore them even after the war when everyone else had switched to shorts.

It reached a point where I simply had to give them up and put on shorts. A pair of long gabardines soaked with the sweat of a typical day on the courts could weigh five pounds, and even more on excessively humid days. How much energy this could cost a player is debatable; that it did cost something is without argument. Rackets are improved over the models that we had, and so are shoes and even socks and shirts and underwear, I suppose. Travel is easier and faster, accommodations are more generous, food is better, and all these things go to help make today's world-wide crop one that is thicker with talent than any other in history.

Nevertheless, I will still maintain that our best amateurs were better than those who have dominated the game more recently. To take an example, consider the case of Gardnar Mulloy. Most people today assume, I think, that Gar and I were of different eras. Actually, Gar is two years older than I am, but he was never able to achieve high rankings in the thirties. Only after Riggs and Parker and Kovacs and myself had left the amateurs could Gar move up in the rankings and achieve Davis Cup status.

I mention this not to disparage Gar in any way, for his many accomplishments, particularly in doubles, speak for themselves. But I do use his career to emphasize how great a tennis generation we had in the years before the war. I would have said that it was the best ever, but now I must qualify that: I believe that open tennis, with its heightened concentration of competition among all the best players, is quickly going to raise the level of play, and that the quality of our time will soon be surpassed by this modern era. Open tournaments will possess not only depth but also a wide range of greatness at the top.

Certainly no one will ever again be able to dominate the game, as Tilden did, without being proficient in every part of the game. I was not a good net player at all in the early stages of my success, because I had developed as a retriever, and I had never ventured near the net. Certainly no one envisioned me as a potentially good doubles player until Gene Mako had the courage to pick me as his doubles partner.

It turned out to be a long and fruitful association, for like almost every good doubles team, we complemented each other, on and off the court. Where I was shy and sometimes still unsure of myself, Gene was confident and positive. He was always outspoken, but he never shot his mouth off unless he was sure that he was right. A newspaperman would come up to Gene and ask him how he felt he was going to do in a certain match, and if Mako honestly felt that he would rout the player mentioned, he would come right out and say it. Then he would do it.

Gene has an encyclopedic mind, especially when it comes to sports. He is one of those fellows who can quote all the batting averages, all the records, all the scores. He was a great sports fan, and he is, as a matter of fact, still involved in tennis—in the court-construction business in Los Angeles.

When we first started playing together he was also the dominant member of our team, for he was a great deal bigger than I was. Gene had matured early and reached his full growth of about a half-inch over six feet when he was only fifteen. Our roles were to change over the years after I grew and became the power player, but at the start of our partnership, when I was still small and still lacked a reliable net game, my assignment was mostly to keep the ball in play and let Mako be the aggressor.

I started off with Gene by playing what most people call the forehand court, or as it is more properly named, the deuce court. (Facing the net, it is the right-hand court, the one into which the first serve of any game is made.) Traditionally, the deuce-court player should concentrate on playing it safe and let the ad-court man go for the winners. The first time we ever played together, big Mako pointed little Budge to the deuce court and ordered, "You play there, and I don't care what you do, but don't miss a ball."

That may sound rather obvious to the uninitiated, but under the circumstances, it made good sense. Gene was merely telling me that it was not my job to worry about winning points, only to keep the ball in play.

Later, after I grew and improved my net game, we switched sides. Wilmer Allison was the person who suggested that we exchange positions, so Mako moved over to the deuce court and assumed the responsibility for sure, steady play. He had all the attributes of the exceptional doubles player. He was consistent, dependable, and he possessed an outstanding net game. He also had a top-notch return of serve, which is extremely important in doubles, where there is always a man at the net to knock any weak return back at you. Mako's reflexes were so quick that I saw matches where our opponents became unnerved and then disheartened when Gene managed somehow to maneuver his body and his racket fast enough to return impossible shots, such as point-blank volleys that most players were content to duck from. We first began beating Allison and John Van Ryn to become the number-one American doubles team, mostly, I am sure, because Gene was able to drive Van Ryn to distraction with his incredible reflex shots. He made such impossible shots regularly and upset any number of outstanding players.

So much of net play, and doubles too, is reflex and quickness. There is seldom the time to get complicated. The simpler your approach to playing the net, the better you should be at that phase of the game.

For instance, close to the net, you should never swing at a volley, as you do with a ground stroke. Be content just to get your racket in the way of the ball. The velocity of the rebound is almost always enough to supply sufficient power. I try to impress this point upon my students by suggesting that they imitate the catching of a ball more than the batting of it—and of course you do not swing at a ball when you are only trying to catch it.

Unfortunately, it is usually difficult to convince new players that they must hardly move the racket. Let's face it—rackets are for swinging, and it is hard to get that impression out of the mind. If a player is determined to volley without a swing, he will often do it against his will. I have even bet some players that they cannot hold the racket still on a volley. They think they do, but they are still swinging, without even knowing it.

Since holding the racket motionless goes against the natural instinct to swing, you must school yourself in thinking the shorter the swing, the better. You usually do have to make some motion with the racket, just to steer the volley, but it need be only the briefest, crispest movement, and you do not have to move your feet at all. Stand with an open stance.

Keep your wrist absolutely as firm as you can, with the racket head pointed up. Keep your wrist low, and then hit down under the ball, getting a slight underspin to your short hit. By holding the racket this way, you will not only help keep your wrist firm but will also limit your natural disposition to swing.

With the low wrist and the short punchy move you make with the racket, you will be better able to deal with the low balls. Remember, the ball is coming fast at you close to the net, and unless you hit down under the ball, you are likely to hit the ball into the net.

Because doubles is such a fast game and so much of the action takes place at the net, you will find that it is wisest to utilize the surest strategy. I took quite awhile to learn this, however. I grew up thinking that the best way to play doubles was to take the additional space that a doubles court provides and concentrate on employing that greater width, shooting for the alleys and trying to force the other team to spread out. It may sound like the best and most logical strategy, but, believe me, it is not. The reverse is. In doubles you should try to hit down the middle. Most people do naturally anyway. Watch any doubles match. I think you'll find that up to ninety per cent of the shots go down the middle.

I certainly didn't know this, though, till the spring of 1936, when I was on the Davis Cup squad practicing at the Chevy Chase Club in Washington. John Van Ryn, Wilmer Allison's long-time partner, had been hurt, and there was some doubt that he would be back in time for our next matches. In practice, we usually played doubles by switching partners, rotating through all the possible combinations on the squad, and Wilmer and I had turned out to be a pretty good pairing. It began to appear that if Van Ryn did not make it back in time, Budge would be partnered with Allison. One day, after a workout, Wilmer called me aside.

"You know, Don," he said. "We work pretty well together, and I have to admit that you're not a bad doubles player, except you're the stupidest damn doubles partner I ever played with. Will you listen to me?"

I said I would.

"Listen, you play every ball you can down the sides."

I nodded.

"Nobody should do that. You should play the ball right down the middle as much as you can."

"You should?" I said.

"Of course you should," Allison said. "I probably shouldn't tell you this, because it's been a big help in me and John beating you and Gene all the time, but if we're going to play together on the team, I guess I can't keep any secrets. Don, in doubles, you just have to hit the ball down the middle most of the time. You've got everything going for you there."

Then Wilmer ticked off the reasons. First of all, he pointed out how the extended doubles net is a full six inches lower in the middle than at the ends. Second, if you are playing the alleys, you can only mis-hit the ball one way and stay alive. If you're off just a little in your shot, the ball is going to fall out.

Third, if you hit a ball down the middle between your two opponents they are likely to freeze for just an instant to see who should best go for the ball. This applies no matter how long a team has played together and no matter how instinctive their play has become. A ball down the middle makes any team hesitate for just the moment that may cost them a worse shot and the point. Ideally, you will even end up with an Alphonse and Gaston act, where neither goes for the ball until it is altogether too late.

Fourth, the opposite is also a possibility. A ball down the middle often brings partners to swordplay, both slashing rackets, trying to make the return. (The next time they'll both probably wait.) Finally, a shot down the middle offers an opponent the least opportunity for him to angle a good return back. Hit a ball into a corner, as I had liked to do, and an opponent then has a good chance to cross-court you cold.

Because you are playing two men instead of one on a court that is only slightly larger, it is not as feasible or as important in doubles to try to get an opponent running. His partner will pick up most shots in half the court anyway. Playing the alleys may win you a few spectacular points now and then, and it is certainly wise on occasion to try to whip a shot down the sideline to keep your opponents honest, but the odds in doubles favor playing the percentages.

It really doesn't matter which kind of style you possess, either. Jack Kramer was powerful and a strong net player, but he seldom went against the percentages. Vinnie Richards was a great doubles player of another sort. He won three United States doubles titles with Tilden and two Challenge Round matches over the French with Norris Williams. As good and as quick as Vinnie was at the net, though, he could not often put a volley away. He would just keep pushing them back at you, though, going with the odds, and often he would win the point.

Many tennis experts believe that the player with the best forehand on a doubles team should play the deuce court, protecting the outside with his forehand. In fact, this is how the term "forehand court" came into use. The player with the best backhand should, according to this thinking, play the ad court. This guards the alleys with good shots and leaves the middle to be defended by two relatively weaker shots. However, two weak shots are not better than one good one, and since almost all the shots go down the middle, that is where I think the very best of your arsenal should be stationed.

With nearly everyone, the most reliable shot is a forehand. Everything else being equal, the partner who owns the better forehand should play the ad court. This puts your best weapon where it will receive the most action. If your opponents then want to shoot for the alleys to take advantage of what is possibly a weak backhand, let them. A doubles team that tries to hit away from the middle is seldom going to win anyway.

After Wilmer Allison tipped me off to the fact that I was playing my shots to the wrong area, my doubles improved immeasurably. Allison and I never did end up playing together after all, though, because Mako and I took over from Allison and Van Ryn as a team. In fact, after I got the word from Wilmer at the Chevy Chase Club, Gene and I just simply swooped by them. For the rest of 1936, Mako and I beat them fourteen straight times, culminating the sweep with a 6-4, 6-2, 6-2 win in the finals of the United States championships at Brookline, Massachusetts, at the Longwood Cricket Club.

The previous year, Wilmer and John had whipped us in the

Longwood finals, and a win in '36 would have given them three legs and permanent possession of the trophy. It was a goal that they truly cared about, and I know exactly how deeply one could care, because the trophy eventually was to be denied Gene and me also. What is more, Allison and Van Ryn had missed the year before going for their third Wimbledon title, losing there in the finals too.

After our match at Longwood, though, Wilmer matched his good sportsmanship with a certain amount of chagrin. "I knew I shouldn't have told you anything about hitting down the middle, Don," he said, smiling and shaking his head.

In a way, that win at Longwood was perhaps the very peak of the Mako-Budge career. It meant that we had defeated what was officially the world's first-ranked team fourteen straight times—and how often does number one lose fourteen straight to anyone in any sport? By that time in '36 there really was no match for Gene and me. Allison and Van Ryn were still much better than any other combination in the world but ours.

The fact that Gene was ranked only fourteenth in the United States in singles may have suggested to some casual fans that I was carrying the team. But that was hardly the case. In fact, I had more than enough hints from some good fans that Gene was hanging onto my coattails. After all, it was said, since Gene was not prospering in singles, the doubles meant more to him than to me. Actually, I honestly think that we shared both the responsibility and the glory in about the same proportions. The official USLTA account of our big win over Allison and Van Ryn noted, "Budge and Mako played a heady, steady resourceful game, getting the best of the breaks but losing few opportunities to press home the advantage they had nearly all the way. The honors go to them equally, for Budge did not dominate the play, and Mako did not have to be carried."

I think the one best match that Gene ever played with me was the next year in the famous Interzone matches with the Germans, the day before my classic battle with Cramm. That was the day I simply could not hit a good overhead and had to keep letting Gene take them whenever he could.

For the last couple of years that we played together, before I turned professional, Gene was often bothered by neuritis, and sometimes it was almost impossible for him to serve. When the neuritis really affected Mako seriously, he had to serve virtually stiff-armed. Overheads became almost as painful and difficult for him to handle as serves, and we were never truly the dominant machine that we had been in 1936. We won Wimbledon, for instance, in '37, but came back to the States after taking the Davis Cup too, and lost to Cramm and Henkel in the finals at Longwood. It was just one of those days when Gene's shoulder was bothering him to such an extent that he was fighting every time to hold his serve, and Cramm and Henkel were both playing superbly.

How Gene managed to get to the finals of Forest Hills in '38 is almost beyond me, except that I know Gene and understand what great spirit he had. He just would not permit himself to think negatively, and I must say that this spirit often caught me and carried me along. The first important match of the first big tournament that we ever played together was in an early round of the National Clay Courts in Chicago when Gene and I were still unranked and unknown. We were coming up against Lefty Bryan and John McDiarmid, the fourth-ranked American team. "Don't worry, Don," Mako assured me. "We can beat them." And of course we did. If Gene had not had such problems with his neuritis, the doubles record we could have left might have been unparalleled.

Gene and I suffered only three major losses, and the most controversial one was the first, at Germantown in 1936 in the Interzone Finals against the Australians. This was just before Mako and I went off on the 14-0 tear against Allison and Van Ryn, and many were still suspicious of our talents, especially of Gene's, for he had little recognition as a singles player.

This was our first major doubles match. We had just replaced Allison and Van Ryn, who had been used as the American team the month before in the opening round of play against the Mexicans at Houston. Allison was getting older, and he was no longer capable of playing three straight days of singles and doubles. In fact, he lost both his singles matches to the Aussies, but I won both of mine, so we needed to win the doubles to move on to the next round in the competition. The Australians put up an outstanding veteran team of Jack Crawford and Adrian Quist, who just happened to be the defending champions of both Wimbledon and France. By almost any measure they were the ranking world team.

What followed, then, was all the more surprising, for the two of us, the rookie Americans, ran them off 6-4, 6-2 in the first two sets. We lost the next one 6-4, but took right off again in the fourth set and built up a 5-4 lead and had Quist down love-30 on his serve. We were two points away from breaking him and winning the match and the odd point in the Interzone. Adrian did come back to win the next point with a smash, but he was still behind 15-30, and the big crowd obviously sensed that an upset was all but complete, when, in the next point, Quist pushed up a little lob that was begging to be anni-hilated.

The lob was right down the middle and presented a perfect ex-ample of how a simple shot that goes directly between two players can cause trouble. I probably should have been the one to make the hit. I was moving up from the ad court, had a clear line on the ball, and would have needed only the simplest of overhead smashes to put the return away and leave Quist at double-match point, 15-40.

Instinctively, though, Gene decided to move over a bit to his left and try a relatively more difficult backhand smash. Certainly, he was the closer, but just as certainly he also had the more difficult shot. And, of course, he missed. It wasn't even close. The ball hit some-where near the top of the handle on his racket, and ended up falling into the bottom of the net. Reprieved, Quist was now back to 30-all. He held his serve, and they broke us in the next game and held for the set, 7-5.

The missed smash made for some controversy. Rightfully, under the circumstances, it was Gene's ball to hit, and more than anything else he was the victim of a windy day. The winds carried the ball crazily off course just enough to cause him to mis-hit it. Secondly, the little lob he tried to hit was really such an easy shot for him that he can hardly be accused of gambling with a bad shot. The truth is, Gene was unfairly blamed out of all proportion for the error. In fact, Gene missed by so much that I can only say that he was mostly unlucky. Maybe it was so easy a shot, even for a backhand smash, that Gene took his eyes off the ball for a crucial instant.

Anyway, what followed was even worse—for both of us. After coming so close to an upset in the fourth set, we probably should have lost all momentum and faded. Instead, we came right back and ripped off a 4-1 lead. What happened next is beyond me. It was not a question of blowing one unlucky shot. We just both disintegrated. Quist and Crawford won the next five games, the set, the match, and, as it turned out, the whole Interzone, by losing only six points to us. We could do nothing right, and one error only served to force another.

The last match we lost together was in '38. It was also against the Aussies—Quist had Bromwich for a new partner now—it was also at Germantown, and it was also the first Davis Cup match, singles or doubles, that I had dropped since the '36 Quist-Crawford debacle. I certainly did not save my best days for Germantown, not in doubles, at any rate.

Just a little while before we had slaughtered Quist and Bromwich 6-3, 6-2, 6-1 at Longwood, we were clearly the top-ranking world team, and the 10,000 people at Germantown assumed we would put the United States ahead 3-0 with an easy win and thus clinch the Cup. When we started off and won the first set at love, it looked like not only a romp but a neat progressive win, for the last four sets we had played against the Aussies had gone 6-3, 6-2, 6-1, 6-0. In hindsight, I guess they had nowhere to go but up. It was 2-2 in the second set, when they began to streak, and they never stopped. Mako and I lost the next three sets 6-3, 6-4, 6-2, as Bromwich in particular got better and better and Gene and I both floundered. Certainly I did not play at all well. I was ill then, you will recall, and I also had probably let myself become preoccupied with my upcoming singles match the next day against Quist. Fortunately, I did win that one to keep the Cup in the United States.

The only other major match that Gene and I lost was that defeat at the hands of Cramm and Henkel in the '37 finals at Longwood. We had beaten Allison and Van Ryn there the year before, and we repeated in '38 too, so had we won in '37 against the Germans we would have won the same trophy that we had denied Allison and Van Ryn. As it was, that trophy was not finally retired until Gar Mulloy and Billy Talbert won it in 1946 with their third win in the tournament.

Incidentally, I'll tell you one thing about trophies, and that is, they sure don't make 'em like they used to. I happened to have about fifteen of my amateur trophies with me in Jamaica, and a silversmith who examined them estimated they were worth $15,000. I have a lot more back in the States too. All the jokes about how amateurs just keep winning the same old bowls and loving cups all of a sudden seemed bearable! However, I am told by players who have won many of the same tournaments that I did that trophies of more recent vintage are not half as heavy and valuable. I don't know quite what that suggests. Maybe the amateurs ought to band together and demand a silver investigation. Or maybe, with all the new gold coming into the game it is no longer worth the effort.

Of course, in doubles, you always had to share the booty, silverware or gold, but I think all tennis players get a special pleasure out of playing *with* someone after being alone so regularly. At various times I played with several other good partners besides Mako. I remember Frankie Parker as being a particularly great doubles partner because he had the special faculty of always being in the proper position.

Frank Sedgman and I made a good team too. Sedgman had enjoyed great doubles success as an amateur some years before, joining first with Bromwich and then with Ken McGregor to beat the United States in the Challenge Round doubles for three years in a row. Shortly after he turned professional in 1953, Sedgman and I were paired together in the pro doubles at Wembley, England. Frank and I were outsiders in the field since we had never played together before, but it turned out that we made the right kind of combination. I played the deuce court and with Frank's good forehand working the middle along with my backhand, we went all the way to the title, swamping Gonzales and Segura 6-2, 6-2, 6-2 in the finals. It was certainly one of the best doubles matches I ever played.

Sedgman possessed one of the great volleys in tennis. He was devastating with it from almost any place on the court, so he was better than most players at being able to charge the net. This had an even greater benefit in doubles. He would just roar in and would seldom get caught in the middle of the court and have to play a half-volley, which is certainly the most defensive and most difficult shot in the game.

Sedgman was also the first top player I had ever seen who gripped the racket for shots with his hand about midway between the eastern grip and the Continental grip. Rosewall and Laver have since also succeeded with this same unusual halfway grip.

There really is no formula for selecting the racket that is best suited to you. For instance, I preferred a racket that was heavier and a racket handle that was larger than almost any other player's. There was no long-thought-out reason involved. It just seemed right to me and it seemed to work.

If you are undecided about which racket to buy, the best method I have found for making a choice is to pick up, handle, and take a few swings with various rackets that are about the size and weight that seem best for you. Then take the one that is the largest and the heaviest. All things being equal, you might as well go for the biggest racket. Remember, though, select the heaviest of the rackets that seem best for you. I do not mean that you should take the heaviest one available.

Once you have played a lot, you should learn to know exactly what racket fits you best. There is, really, only the difference of a few ounces between the very heaviest and the lightest rackets, but just a smidgen of weight or an eighth of an inch in the handle size can seem gigantic if you are used to another model.

I remember one time at Newport when I was standing behind one court there, watching Frank Shields play. Shields was a big fellow, but he played with a racket that weighed about thirteen and three quarter ounces, a weight close to the average. I preferred a racket of fifteen and a half ounces, with a four and seven-eighths inch handle (though now I am down to fifteen ounces and up to five inches on the grip).

Anyway, while I was idly watching Shields play, he managed to hit a run of bad luck and broke two rackets in quick succession. What's more, it seemed that he had broken another racket earlier in the match. Frank was well on his way to a win in his match, and rather than go through all the trouble of looking around for a racket exactly his size Frank just called back to me and asked if he could borrow one of mine to finish the match with. I flipped him a racket.

Frank played two points with it, and then threw it right back to me. "Good grief, Don," he said, "I can't play with this. I don't even see where you get the strength to carry it around."

Of course, my big cudgel only weighed an ounce and three quarters more than Frank's neat little bat, and that difference is hardly much more than a few pages in this book. But swinging it and raising it over the head to serve for a few sets, or even a few points, can make the ounce and three quarters feel like substantially more. Great powers of adjustment are required when anyone who plays regularly switches rackets.

While many diverse doubles combinations have worked well, the ideal pair would match one right-hander and one left-hander. This arrangement gives any team a startling advantage. First of all, and perhaps more important than it might seem, with such a team neither player will ever have to serve staring up into the sun. Secondly, when a southpaw is included, the two partners can cover the middle with two forehands. The left-hander should always play the deuce court to give him the forehand down the middle.

The best lefty-righty combination I ever saw was the team of Johnny Doeg and George Lott, who won at Longwood in 1929 and 1930. Doeg, of course, had the devastating serve, while Lott possessed a perfect complementing temperament and general doubles-play ability. He won the United States title three other times with two different partners.

Although players are usually matched with partners who bring different abilities to the unit—one hard hitter, one all-court scrambler is the typical arrangement—a few doubles teams have succeeded by featuring players who were practically identical in style. The classic such pair were the Kinsey brothers, Howard and Robert, who won the '24 United States title and many other championships with the one basic strategy of wearing the opposition out with lobs.

The lob is used more in doubles than in singles, for one of its main purposes is to force at least one member of the opposition away from the net, and, of course, there is more net play in doubles. In my own case, and in that of most hard hitters, I viewed the lob as little more than an auxiliary shot, to be hit almost always as a defensive maneuver.

The rare times that I would go for an offensive lob were when I found my opponents right smack on top of the net and I felt that they just could never get back in time to retrieve a lob. I would hit up and over the ball, giving the shot a topspin that should carry the ball away on a big long bounce. But the majority of the lobs I hit were of the defensive variety, when I had been placed in a difficult position and was trying to buy time to get back into the point. A defensive lob should be hit high and given underspin. Hit it with the racket face beveled rather like a nine-iron in golf.

The players who possessed the most dangerous lobs were rarely big hitters, but were usually the little retriever types. Riggs, Grant, and Bromwich—each included the lob as a major part of his arsenal. Each understood when to employ the lob, regularly or sparingly or not at all, depending on the circumstances. Bromwich—and Riggs too—was a master at hitting a lob and sending you back from the net, chipping a shot to bring you up close again, then back with a lob, and so on till your tongue fell out. He could make you feel like a yo-yo, and even if he lost the point, you had paid for it in energy.

Another advantage to the lob is that it forces the opponent to make a difficult return shot—the overhead. That is a tiring shot to hit, too, for you must reach up, and often it also means staring up into the sun. Any lob that falls short will probably give your opponent a chance to win the point with an easy smash. On balance, the lob is a calculated risk. You leave a great deal of your fate in your opponent's hands. If players could hit overheads as well as they can hit lobs, there would be no more lobs.

Certainly, though, I have a great deal more respect for the lob than for the drop shot, which is really a nothing ball, undersliced and hit with no pace whatsoever. There are times, when your opponent is far back, when tactics do indeed suggest a drop shot. Unfortunately, too many players become drop-shot happy and lose all discretion in the matter.

I say that you should never attempt a drop shot if you are far back yourself, by or behind the baseline. It is too precise a shot to try from such a distance. The odds are against you. Secondly, never under any circumstances try a drop shot unless you are fairly certain that it will win the point or that you can really tire your opponent by making him run a great distance. It is never a shot to be used to parry with. Employ it only when you are very sure of the immediate value of the shot and of your ability to execute it.

Another ploy that is too often tried in doubles is poaching. For those unfamiliar with the term, it refers to the player at the net trying to surprise the opposition by shifting to the middle as his partner serves. Ideally for the poacher, the return will come right back to him in the middle, and he will have an easy shot for the point. Poaching is sometimes a worthwhile tactic, if only occasionally to shake up the opposition and make them wonder. The threat of poaching is, then, perhaps of greater value than the act.

Poachers themselves, like drop-shot addicts, usually overdo it, particularly if they are successful at it early in the match. If you suspect that you have a confirmed poacher playing against you, the best way to handle him is to slam a few returns right back at him early. In other words, make *him* think too. If he gets the idea that you like to return serve where he should be, he is surely going to be less disposed to rambling about. Poachers do not like to be embarrassed. Catch them red-handed once, and they often will not try it again.

The Budge Poachers' Survey also offers this advice if you really want to try to catch a poacher in the act. A confirmed poacher, I am convinced after years of study, is most likely to poach on the first serve of an important point. When you reach a spot in any match that seems to meet these qualifications, hit the return nice and easy to where the poacher should be if he were playing it straight. I'll bet he isn't. I'll bet he's in the middle of the court, trying, in embarrassment, to avoid looking at his partner.

Incidentally, when you do poach yourself, keep in mind that the best time to do it is when you are at the net in the ad court. If you are a right-hander, it is only from the ad-court side that you possess a long forehand reach. Of course, you must occasionally poach from the deuce court to keep the opposition confused, but keep such moves to a minimum.

Generally, I would also advise that men players would probably be wise to poach more when they are playing mixed doubles. I do not suggest that any male should make great changes in his doubles game when he is playing mixed; on the contrary, I think the best way to play mixed doubles is to go at it the same way you would playing men's doubles. When playing with a good lady partner, do not try to dominate the court. In the long run, the percentages—so vital to doubles—will almost surely turn against you. The exceptions would be more poaching, as I said, and moving over to take optional overheads on a regular basis. Otherwise, play your side of the court and let your lady partner play hers. This is not only strategically advisable but also manages to keep the war of the sexes from escalating.

If you are ever lucky enough to have a partner with the abilities of someone like Alice Marble, just consider yourself blessed and don't worry about a thing. Alice was any man's favorite doubles partner. In a period of five years, she won the United States Mixed Doubles title four times, on each occasion with a different man—Mako, Budge, Harry Hopman of Australia, and Bobby Riggs. Mrs. Sarah Palfrey Fabyan, another outstanding woman player, and I teamed up to take the title in that one year Alice didn't, and while Sarah was a valued partner, there was no one to compare with Alice. She could handle overheads and almost any other shot as proficiently as all but the best of men. There was no need to make any compensations on the court on her behalf.

In mixed doubles, then, as in any phase of the game or at almost any level, we return to the fact that doubles is a game of percentages and a game of the net. You must take and hold the net to win at doubles, and the best way to do that is to keep your opposition back away from the net.

So, volley deep, playing to the person who is farther back. Generally, if a player must hit a shot, he is less able to move up. Hit to the man at the net only when you can whack a good shot at his feet, and you usually need a nice high shot to manage this. Don't take chances, and don't forget to play deep and down the middle instead of to the sides.

Doubles is an exciting game to watch, more exciting in many instances than is singles. It is also almost certainly a more enjoyable game to play, for it manages to retain most of the hard competitive advantages of singles, while adding the fun and satisfaction that comes with teamwork. Besides, doubles makes it possible to play tennis for just about as long as you live, and that in itself is sufficient to recommend it.

Epilogue

Jack Kramer was waiting there at the airport to meet us when my wife Lori and I arrived in London for the 1968 Wimbledon. It was thirty years almost to the day since last I had played there—thirty years since the Grand Slam, thirty years since I had turned professional. Literally a whole generation had passed, for now I was to play in the senior division (forty-five years and over). To play once again on the Wimbledon grass, I would have entered any category at all. It had been too long. "Welcome back," Jack said, taking my hand.

I went out to the courts for the first time the next day after practicing at the Queen's Club. Lori had never been to Wimbledon before, so that I think that heightened the experience even more as we passed onto the grounds, through the majestic iron gates that immortalize the famous Doherty brothers, who had been two of Great Britain's earliest champions. The broad walk was before us, with the courts and the lawns, the scoreboard and concession counters set along the sides of the wide promenade. They were still selling strawberries and cream. The lawns were as lush as ever—even more so, perhaps, for this had been a rainy time even for England— and the bright flowers were everywhere, the hydrangeas, fuchsias, and roses. I looked up at the stadium that holds Centre Court and backs onto the main walkway. The ivy seemed to cling even higher to the walls. Maybe that was the only difference in the place. If Wimbledon had changed at all, perhaps it was only that it was greener still—the grass, the ivy, even the towels.

Wimbledon is really the name of a suburb of London where the courts are located, just as Forest Hills is but a section of a New York City borough that happens to contain the West Side Tennis Club. Wimbledon is technically the All-England Lawn Tennis and Croquet Club. It used to be the All-England Croquet and Lawn Tennis Club, but if tennis has moved to the forefront, do not be deceived that croquet—"krokie" the British call it, instead of "krokay"—is held lightly. It is not.

But then, I don't know of anything at Wimbledon that is approached in a half-hearted way. If it cannot be done right, it is not done at all. Senior play was added to the schedule only in the last few years, when it was decided that seniors could be accorded the free tickets and chauffeured limousines and all other courtesies due men's and ladies' players. As a senior competitor, I found that I and all my contemporaries were treated with the same degree of attention and politeness as were Rod Laver and Billie Jean King. The only senior play yet permitted is men's doubles. Men's singles and senior ladies' play will be added only when the Club is sure that such added competitors can be properly treated.

A cocktail party was held for the senior players and other members of the old guard at the Club manager's lodge one evening late in the tournament. It was a typically thoughtful gesture, and many of us were on hand to reminisce and laugh together. I had learned from the German Davis Cup captain, Heinrich Kleinscroth, that Gottfried von Cramm might fly in for this affair and for the last few days of the tournament, but he was unable to make it. Fred Perry, Bunny Austin, and Mary Hardwicke Hare and her husband, Charlie Hare, were there, helping represent the host country. Bobby Riggs, Jack Kramer, and I were among the American visitors.

Bobby and Jack had both hoped to play in the senior doubles, but freak circumstances had eliminated them both. The night before play began, Bobby had a heavy glass hotel door blow shut on his thumb. The door crashed so hard on Bobby's thumb that it nearly severed it altogether.

Jack and I, as I mentioned earlier, had planned to play as a team, but then he was ruled out of the action by some legislation that, it seemed to me, was only technically applicable in his case. During the twenties, when the United States met France in the Challenge Round at Paris one year, Bill Tilden began writing some articles about the matches for a daily newspaper. Tennis officials felt that, as he was playing, Tilden was not only improperly capitalizing on his good amateur name, but that he was also devising an unfair psychological advantage, since he could run down his opponents in the local press before meeting them. It was decreed that no amateur could both report and play.

The rule has been maintained since then, and was broadened to include all in Open play. Since Kramer had agreed to appear as a commentator on the BBC, the rule was applied against him, even though he was only appearing in the Veterans' Doubles. This seemed to be an unnecessarily strict interpretation to many people, and efforts were promptly begun to waive the ruling in the case of senior players. The change could not, however, be effected in time for the '68 Wimbledon, and Jack was barred.

Losing Jack as a partner was certainly a keen disappointment, but I found an able replacement in John Faunce, a fellow Californian who has taught many Hollywood personalities how to play tennis. John and I had played together before, and had three days of good practice at Queen's before our first-round match, so we were pretty familiar with each other when play started. We had a good first match too, beating two Irish gentlemen, J. J. Fitzgibbon and B. A. Haughton, 6-1, 6-3.

The next day we started off well again against a team made up of a couple of old friends from Portland, Oregon—Emory Neale, the United States senior singles champion, and Sammy Lee. Sammy and I had played against each other often thirty-five years ago in the Juniors. We had come the full circle. Faunce and I had Neale and Lee 4-2 in the first set, and John had 40-love on his serve, game point at 5-2, when somehow we let the game get away from us. Neale and Lee took four straight games for the set, and then moved ahead 5-1 in the second set before John and I rallied to come back to 5-4. But we ran out of luck, and lost the next game and the match.

As much as I regretted that Jack could not play, I know that many fans were even more dismayed that they did not get the opportunity to see Jack and me play together. I think that Jack's absence even removed some of the interest from the senior play, but still, the Number One Court, which seats 7000, was filled to a standing-room capacity for the senior finals. Jaroslav Drobny partnered with Al Martini to beat Gar Mulloy and Sammy Match to take the title. And I noticed that Laver and Lew Hoad were interested enough to join the crowd in attendance.

Of course, in 1968 no single match in any division could mean so much as the primary fact that at last pros and amateurs were playing each other in this greatest tennis place of all. Since 1877, when the Wimbledon championships were started only four years after the game of tennis itself was devised, they have paced the game, and in 1968 the entire experience seemed more impressive than ever. Above all, however, is the fact that when Rod Laver walked off the court after defeating Tony Roche in the finals, he left as the undisputed champion of the world. There can never again be any doubt that the man who wins Wimbledon is, at that time, the greatest player in the world.

I was not too surprised by how many good players were on hand and that so many upsets occurred, a fact that was accented even more two months later at Forest Hills when Arthur Ashe, still an amateur, won the first United States Open. As I have said, tennis has such great depth now that it is a healthy sign of the whole sport's development that good, rising amateurs can beat some of the lesser professionals. In the over-all picture, I do feel, however, that Ashe's victory as an amateur in the first United States Open will turn out to be something of an exception. I think that Arthur's game rose to the level so many of us thought he could obtain at just the right time.

Arthur's victory was magnificent for him, but there were so many fine performances by American players that it is possible to believe that all of American tennis is moving out of the doldrums after so many years. Dennis Ralston went out gamely with a painful, debilitating injury against Rosewall in the quarters at Forest Hills, but he gave Laver much his hardest battle at Wimbledon, losing only after five hard sets in the quarter-finals. Ashe not only won at Forest

Hills but also made the semis at Wimbledon, and Clark Graebner reached the semis before losing in both tournaments.

Teaming with Frankie Parker, I got to the quarter-finals in the Senior Doubles at Forest Hills myself, which was at least an improvement over my Wimbledon showing. The lion's share of the credit for our team should probably go to Frankie, though. He was, as ever, all over the court and invariably in the right place. Frankie still manages to play virtually every day, and was in great shape. We were defeated by Bobby Riggs and Pancho Segura, who then went on to the finals, where Gar Mulloy and Torsten Johansson edged them.

Pancho was definitely the dominant man on the court in our match. He probably plays even more than Parker does, but perhaps even more important he is five years younger than Frankie, and that tells in senior play. His performance and Parker's taught me one thing: that I should not play again in the seniors if I cannot get in the neccessary preliminary practice. It was a simple lack of conditioning that caused me to fall short. There are too many good players competing in the event who play all the time, so that someone like me cannot expect to drift in cold and play as well as he would like to. If I'm in the line-up next year or any time in the future, I don't know whether I'll have any more success, but I will be in better condition.

I know it comes as no secret to anyone old enough to vote, that each birthday makes it harder to get in shape and stay there. It may be of some consolation to those of you who have tried to stay in shape, and sometimes failed at it, to know that playing tennis was still part of my livelihood into middle age, but that I had trouble disciplining myself and exercising the kind of will power that was so easy to exert when I was younger.

There are no secrets to staying in shape well enough to be healthy and play good tennis as you get older. My best advice, and that which I try to follow, is to at least be regular in finding exercise. You can jog or run in the winter just as well as in the summer. The stomach-muscle exercises that I described in Chapter 4 are always profitable. Since our stomachs cause us more trouble as we get older, the exercises to help keep a trim stomach should never be forgotten. But let's be realistic. If nothing else, at least remember the old gag and get some exercise pushing yourself away from the table or the bar. That's half the battle right there.

As a final tip, if you want to be in better shape to play tennis, remember that tennis is pretty good exercise itself, and practice can improve your condition and your game.

Playing at Wimbledon and Forest Hills in 1968 gave me the opportunity to see a great deal of the best tennis, and I was particularly and pleasantly surprised to see that so many of the players, Americans and otherwise, displayed such a marked improvement with their ground strokes. This vital phase of the game has picked up considerably in the last few years, and it is a welcome improvement. Laver's victory over Roche in the Wimbledon finals appeared so impressive primarily because Roche was able to return service with much less than his usual proficiency, and ground strokes are, of course, the major function of return of service.

Normally, Roche's return of service had been considerably better than it was that day. Until recently, the return of serve had been the weakest part of the best players' games, but now Roche and his contemporaries have brought ground strokes back into fashion, so that suddenly we are surprised when we *don't* see the good return. So many people raved at the powerful serves that Ashe and Graebner showed, but the truth is that their improved return of service was at least as responsible for their strings of victories. Ashe also has developed an outstanding topspin backhand that caught many of his opponents digging in vain at their shoe tops for the fast-dropping shots.

Indeed, there are just so many good players now that the ones who want to be best must abandon the simple serve-and-volley strategy and develop the ground strokes that can give them a full-court game. The reason I do not believe that Billie Jean King can be ranked with Alice Marble and Maureen Connolly and Pauline Betz Addie and others of the greatest of women's players is that Billie Jean's ground strokes remain rather flimsy. She tends to rely on the big serve-and-volley game too much, in the same way that the best male players of a decade ago depended upon that type of offense.

Billie Jean won her third Wimbledon, though, and she made a

lovely partner with Laver when they led the traditional first dance at the Wimbledon Ball at Grosvenor House Saturday night after the tournament was finished. The honor of having the first dance with the ladies' champion was one that I never enjoyed. The first year I won, Helen Wills Moody was the women's champion, but she had to leave London right after the tournament. The next year I won again, but then I had commitments and had to leave England before the ball.

The final ball is as much fun and as exciting as any part of Wimbledon, but in 1968, the year that all of tennis, amateur and professional, came together at last, there was a special thrill for me in returning to be part of it all. Wimbledon touches all of us in tennis, each differently, perhaps, but each deeply.

Back home now, I stand before the display of my trophies, fought for and won over the years. There is my first loving cup, standing proudly in the center of the glittering array . . . and I recall the words of Rudyard Kipling inscribed over the players' entrance to the Centre Court, the last thing you see before you step out onto the fabled grass:

"If you can meet with triumph and disaster . . ."

I hear my mother's voice speaking to a complaining fifteen-year-old who has just suffered a defeat: "Don, honey," she is saying, "don't make excuses. That boy just plain played better than you did today. Work hard and maybe you'll be the winner next time. But no belly-aching when you lose!" That little silver-plated cup looms now as large and as beautiful as the heavy, ornate Renshaw cups that are my Wimbledon trophies as they gleam side by side in the case.

"and treat those two impostors just the same. . . ."

Thanks again, Ma, for helping me begin to know the meaning of those inspiring words long before I ever carried them with me out onto the Centre Court, and on into life.

APPENDIX

United States Grass Championships, Finals
(*Since 1930*)

1930 JOHN DOEG d. Francis X. Shields, 10-8, 1-6, 6-4, 16-14
1931 ELLSWORTH VINES d. George Lott, 7-9, 6-3, 9-7, 7-5
1932 VINES d. Henri Cochet, 6-4, 6-4, 6-4
1933 FRED PERRY d. Jack Crawford, 6-3, 11-13, 4-6, 6-0, 6-1
1934 PERRY d. Wilmer Allison, 6-4, 6-3, 3-6, 1-6, 8-6
      Don Budge, unseeded, lost to Vernon Kirby, 4-6, 6-4, 6-4, 6-4, in fourth round
1935 WILMER ALLISON d. Sidney Wood, 6-2, 6-2, 6-3
      Budge, No. 2 United States seed, lost to Bitsy Grant, 6-4, 6-4, 5-7, 6-3, in quarter-finals
1936 PERRY d. Budge, 2-6, 6-2, 8-6, 1-6, 10-8
1937 DON BUDGE d. Gottfried von Cramm, 6-1, 7-9, 6-1, 3-6, 6-1
1938 BUDGE d. Gene Mako, 6-3, 6-8, 6-2, 6-1
1939 BOBBY RIGGS d. Welby Van Horn, 6-4, 6-2, 6-4
1940 DON McNEILL d. Riggs, 8-6, 6-8, 6-3, 7-5
1941 RIGGS d. Frank Kovacs, 5-7, 6-1, 6-3, 6-3
1942 TED SCHROEDER d. Frank Parker, 8-6, 7-5, 3-6, 4-6, 6-2
1943 JOE HUNT d. Jack Kramer, 6-3, 6-8, 10-8, 6-0
1944 FRANK PARKER d. Bill Talbert, 6-4, 3-6, 6-3, 6-3
1945 PARKER d. Talbert, 14-12, 6-1, 6-2
1946 JACK KRAMER d. Tom Brown, 9-7, 6-3, 6-0
1947 KRAMER d. Parker, 4-6, 2-6, 6-1, 6-0, 6-3
1948 PANCHO GONZALES d. Eric Sturgess, 6-2, 6-3, 14-12
1949 GONZALES d. Schroeder, 16-18, 2-6, 6-1, 6-2, 6-4
1950 ART LARSEN d. Herb Flam, 6-3, 4-6, 5-7, 6-4, 6-3
1951 FRANK SEDGMAN d. Vic Seixas, 6-4, 6-1, 6-1
1952 SEDGMAN d. Gardnar Mulloy, 6-1, 6-2, 6-3
1953 TONY TRABERT d. Seixas, 6-3, 6-2, 6-3
1954 VIC SEIXAS d. Rex Hartwig, 3-6, 6-2, 6-4, 6-4
1955 TRABERT d. Ken Rosewall, 9-7, 6-3, 6-3
1956 KEN ROSEWALL d. Lew Hoad, 4-6, 6-2, 6-3, 6-3
1957 MAL ANDERSON d. Ashley Cooper, 10-8, 7-5, 6-4
1958 ASHLEY COOPER d. Anderson, 6-2, 3-6, 4-6, 10-8, 8-6

1959 NEALE FRASER d. Alex Olmedo, 6-3, 5-7, 6-2, 6-4
1960 FRASER d. Rod Laver, 6-4, 6-4, 10-8
1961 ROY EMERSON d. Laver, 7-5, 6-3, 6-2
1962 ROD LAVER d. Emerson, 6-2, 6-4, 5-7, 6-4
1963 RAFAEL OSUNA d. Frank Froehling, 7-5, 6-4, 6-2
1964 EMERSON d. Fred Stolle, 6-4, 6-1, 6-4
1965 MANUEL SANTANA d. Cliff Drysdale, 6-2, 7-9, 7-5, 6-1
1966 FRED STOLLE d. John Newcombe, 4-6, 12-10, 6-3, 6-4
1967 JOHN NEWCOMBE d. Clark Graebner, 6-4, 6-4, 8-6
1968 National Amateur*
     ARTHUR ASHE d. Bob Lutz, 4-6, 6-3, 8-10, 6-0, 6-4
     National Open
     ASHE d. Tom Okker, 14-12, 5-7, 6-3, 3-6, 6-3

United States Professional Champions

1927 VINCENT RICHARDS d. Howard Kinsey, 11-9, 6-4, 6-3, Notlek Tennis Courts, New York, September 25
1928 RICHARDS d. Karel Kozeluh, 8-6, 6-3, 0-6, 6-2, Forest Hills, New York, September 29
1929 KAREL KOZELUH d. Richards, 6-4, 6-4, 4-6, 4-6, 7-5, Forest Hills, New York, September 28
1930 RICHARDS d. Kozeluh, 2-6, 10-8, 6-3, 6-4, Forest Hills, New York, September 20
1931 BILL TILDEN d. Richards, 7-5, 6-2, 6-1, Forest Hills, New York, July 10
1932 KOZELUH d. Hans Nusslein, 6-2, 6-2, 7-5, South Shore Country Club, Chicago, August 26
1933 RICHARDS d. Frank Hunter, 6-3, 6-0, 6-2, Westchester Country Club, Rye, New York, October 3
1934 HANS NUSSLEIN d. Kozeluh, 6-4, 6-2, 1-6, 7-5, South Shore Country Club, Chicago, August 26
1935 TILDEN d. Kozeluh, 0-6, 6-1, 6-4, 0-6, 6-4, Terrace Club, Brooklyn, New York, September 16
1936 JOSEPH WHALEN d. Charles Wood, 4-6, 4-6, 6-3, 6-2, 6-3, Tudor City Tennis Courts, New York, July 17
1937 KOZELUH d. Bruce Barnes, 6-2, 6-3, 4-6, 4-6, 6-1, White Sulphur Springs, West Virginia, October 18
1938 FRED PERRY d. Barnes, 6-3, 6-2, 6-4, Arena, Chicago, October 2
1939 ELLSWORTH VINES d. Perry, 8-6, 6-8, 6-1, 20-18, Beverly Hills Tennis Club, Beverly Hills, October 22

* Played at Brookline, Mass. All other tournaments played at Forest Hills, New York.

1940 DON BUDGE d. Perry, 6-3, 5-7, 6-4, 6-3, Town and Country Ten-
      nis Club, Chicago, September 29
1941 PERRY d. Dick Skeen, 6-4, 6-8, 6-2, 6-3, Town and Country Ten-
      nis Club, Chicago, June 1
1942 BUDGE d. Bobby Riggs, 6-2, 6-2, 6-2, Forest Hills, New York,
      July 4
1943 LT. BRUCE BARNES d. John Nogrady, 6-1, 7-9, 7-5, 4-6, 6-3,
      Officers Club, Fort Knox, Kentucky, October 10
1944 No tournament
1945 WELBY VAN HORN d. Nogrady, 6-4, 6-2, 6-2, Rip's Courts, New
      York, July 1
1946 RIGGS d. Budge, 6-3, 6-1, 6-1, Forest Hills, New York, July 14
1947 RIGGS d. Budge, 3-6, 6-3, 10-8, 4-6, 6-3, Forest Hills, New York,
      June 22
1948 JACK KRAMER d. Riggs, 14-12, 6-2, 3-6, 6-3, Forest Hills, New
      York, June 20
1949 RIGGS d. Budge, 9-7, 3-6, 6-3, 7-5, Forest Hills, New York,
      June 28
1950 PANCHO SEGURA d. Frank Kovacs, 6-4, 1-6, 8-6, 4-4, default
      (cramps), Cleveland Skating Club, Cleveland, June 12
1951 SEGURA d. Pancho Gonzales, 6-3, 6-4, 6-2, Forest Hills, New
      York, July 4
1952 SEGURA d. Gonzales, 3-6, 6-4, 3-6, 6-4, 6-0, Lakewood Park,
      Cleveland, June 7
1953 PANCHO GONZALES d. Budge, 4-6, 6-4, 7-5, 6-2, Lakewood Park,
      Cleveland, June 21
1954 GONZALES d. Frank Sedgman, 6-3, 9-7, 3-6, 6-2, Arena, Cleve-
      land, May 2
1955 GONZALES d. Segura, 21-16, 19-21, 21-8, 20-22, 21-19 (VASSS),
      Arena, Cleveland, April 2
1956 GONZALES d. Segura, 21-15, 13-21, 21-14, 22-20 (VASSS),
      Arena, Cleveland, April 6
1957 GONZALES d. Segura, 6-3, 3-6, 7-5, 6-1, Arena, Cleveland,
      April 12
1958 GONZALES d. Lew Hoad, 3-6, 4-6, 14-12, 6-1, 6-4, Arena, Cleve-
      land, May 5
1959 GONZALES d. Hoad, 6-4, 6-2, 6-4, Arena, Cleveland, April 26
1960 ALEX OLMEDO d. Tony Trabert, 7-5, 6-4, Arena, Cleveland,
      May 29
1961 GONZALES d. Sedgman, 6-3, 7-5, Arena, Cleveland, May 3
1962 BUTCH BUCHHOLZ d. Segura, 6-4, 6-3, 6-4, Arena, Cleveland,
      May 5
1963 KEN ROSEWALL d. Rod Laver, 6-4, 6-2, 6-2, Forest Hills, New
      York, June 29
1964 ROD LAVER d. Gonzales, 4-6, 6-3, 7-5, 6-4, Longwood Cricket
      Club, Boston, July 12

1965   ROSEWALL d. Laver, 6-4, 6-3, 6-3, Longwood Cricket Club, Boston, July 19
1966   LAVER d. Rosewall, 6-4, 4-6, 6-2, 8-10, 6-3, Longwood Cricket Club, Boston, July 17
1967   LAVER d. Andres Gimeno, 4-6, 6-4, 6-3, 7-5, Longwood Cricket Club, Boston, July 17
1968   LAVER d. John Newcombe, 6-4, 6-4, 9-7, Longwood Cricket Club, Boston, September 10

United States Men's Doubles Championships
(*Since 1930*)

1930   GEORGE LOTT and JOHN DOEG d. John Van Ryn and Wilmer Allison, 6-3, 4-6, 15-13, 6-4
1931   JOHN VAN RYN and WILMER ALLISON d. Berkeley Bell and Gregory Mangin, 6-4, 8-6, 6-3
1932   ELLSWORTH VINES and KEITH GLEDHILL d. Van Ryn and Allison, 6-4, 6-3, 6-2
1933   LOTT and LESTER STOEFEN d. Frank Shields and Frank Parker, 11-13, 9-7, 9-7, 6-3
1934   LOTT and STOEFEN d. Van Ryn and Allison, 6-4, 9-7, 3-6, 6-4
1935   VAN RYN and ALLISON d. Don Budge and Gene Mako, 6-2, 6-3, 2-6, 3-6, 6-1
1936   DON BUDGE and GENE MAKO d. Van Ryn and Allison, 6-4, 6-2, 6-4
1937   GOTTFRIED VON CRAMM and HENNER HENKEL d. Budge and Mako, 6-4, 7-5, 6-4
1938   BUDGE and MAKO d. Adrian Quist and John Bromwich, 6-3, 6-2, 6-1
1939   ADRIAN QUIST and JOHN BROMWICH d. Jack Crawford and Harry Hopman, 8-6, 6-1, 6-4
1940   JACK KRAMER and TED SCHROEDER d. Gardnar Mulloy and Henry Prussoff, 6-4, 8-6, 9-7
1941   KRAMER and SCHROEDER d. Mulloy and Wayne Sabin, 9-7, 6-4, 6-2
1942   GARDNAR MULLOY and BILL TALBERT d. Schroeder and Sidney Wood, 9-7, 7-5, 6-1
1943   KRAMER and FRANK PARKER d. Talbert and David Freeman, 6-2, 6-4, 6-4
1944   DON MCNEILL and BOB FALKENBURG d. Talbert and Pancho Segura, 7-5, 6-4, 3-6, 6-1

1945 MULLOY and TALBERT d. Falkenburg and Jack Tuero, 12-10, 8-10, 12-10, 6-2
1946 MULLOY and TALBERT d. McNeill and Frank Guernsey, 3-6, 6-4, 2-6, 6-3, 20-18
1947 KRAMER and SCHROEDER d. Talbert and Bill Sidwell, 6-4, 7-5, 6-3
1948 MULLOY and TALBERT d. Schroeder and Parker, 1-6, 9-7, 6-3, 3-6, 9-7
1949 BILL SIDWELL and BROMWICH d. Frank Sedgman and George Worthington, 6-4, 6-0, 6-1
1950 BROMWICH and FRANK SEDGMAN d. Mulloy and Talbert, 7-5, 8-6, 3-6, 6-1
1951 SEDGMAN and KEN McGREGOR d. Mervyn Rose and Don Candy, 10-8, 4-6, 6-4, 7-5
1952 VIC SEIXAS and MERVYN ROSE d. Sedgman and McGregor, 3-6, 10-8, 10-8, 6-8, 8-6
1953 ROSE and REX HARTWIG d. Mulloy and Talbert, 6-4, 4-6, 6-2, 6-4
1954 SEIXAS and TONY TRABERT d. Lew Hoad and Ken Rosewall, 3-6, 6-4, 8-6, 6-3
1955 KOSEI KAMO and ATSUSHI MIYAGI d. Gerald Moss and William Quillian, 6-2, 6-3, 3-6, 1-6, 6-4
1956 LEW HOAD and KEN ROSEWALL d. Seixas and Ham Richardson, 6-2, 6-2, 3-6, 6-4
1957 ASHLEY COOPER and NEALE FRASER d. Mulloy and Budge Patty, 4-6, 6-3, 9-7, 6-3
1958 ALEX OLMEDO and HAM RICHARDSON d. Sam Giammalva and Barry MacKay, 3-6, 6-3, 6-4, 6-4
1959 FRASER and ROY EMERSON d. Olmedo and Butch Buchholz, 3-6, 6-3, 5-7, 6-4, 7-5
1960 FRASER and EMERSON d. Rod Laver and Bob Mark, 9-7, 6-2, 6-4
1961 CHUCK McKINLEY and DENNIS RALSTON d. Rafael Osuna and Antonio Palafox, 6-3, 6-4, 2-6, 13-11
1962 RAFAEL OSUNA and ANTONIO PALAFOX d. McKinley and Ralston, 6-4, 10-12, 1-6, 9-7, 6-3
1963 McKINLEY and RALSTON d. Osuna and Palafox, 9-7, 4-6, 5-7, 6-3, 11-9
1964 McKINLEY and RALSTON d. Michael Sangster and Graham Stillwell, 6-3, 6-2, 6-4
1965 EMERSON and FRED STOLLE d. Frank Froehling and Charlie Pasarell, 6-4, 10-12, 7-5, 6-3
1966 EMERSON and STOLLE d. Ralston and Clark Graebner, 6-4, 6-4, 6-4
1967 JOHN NEWCOMBE and TONY ROCHE d. Bill Bowrey and Owen Davidson, 6-8, 9-7, 6-3, 6-3
1968 Amateur

Bob Lutz and Stan Smith d. Bob Hewitt and Ray Moore, 6-4,
6-4, 9-7
Open
Lutz and Smith d. Arthur Ashe and Andres Gimeno, 11-9, 6-1,
7-5

United States Mixed Doubles Championships

(*Since 1930*)

1930 Edith Cross and Wilmer Allison d. Marjorie Morrill and
      Frank Shields, 6-4, 6-4
1931 Betty Nuthall and George Lott d. Mrs. Lawrence Harper
      and Allison, 6-3, 6-3
1932 Sarah Palfrey and Fred Perry d. Helen Jacobs and Ellsworth
      Vines, 6-3, 7-5
1933 Elizabeth Ryan and Ellsworth Vines d. Miss Palfrey and
      Lott, 11-9, 6-1
1934 Helen Jacobs and Lott d. Miss Ryan and Lester Stoefen, 4-6,
      13-11, 6-2
1935 Mrs. Sarah Palfrey Fabyan and Enrique Maier d. Kath-
      erine Stammers and Roderich Menzel, 8-6, 6-4
1936 Alice Marble and Gene Mako d. Mrs. Fabyan and Don Budge,
      6-3, 6-2
1937 Mrs. Sarah Palfrey Fabyan and Don Budge d. Mme. Sylvia
      Henrotin and Yvon Petra, 6-2, 8-10, 6-0
1938 Miss Marble and Budge d. Thelma Coyne and John Bromwich,
      6-1, 6-2
1939 Miss Marble and Harry Hopman d. Mrs. Fabyan and Elwood
      Cooke, 9-7, 6-1
1940 Miss Marble and Bobby Riggs d. Dorothy Bundy and Jack
      Kramer, 9-7, 6-1
1941 Mrs. Sarah Palfrey Cooke and Jack Kramer d. Pauline
      Betz and Riggs, 4-6, 6-4, 6-4
1942 Louise Brough and Ted Schroeder d. Mrs. Patricia Todd and
      Alejo Russell, 3-6, 6-1, 6-4
1943 Margaret Osborne and Bill Talbert d. Pauline Betz and
      Pancho Segura, 10-8, 6-4
1944 Miss Osborne and Talbert d. Dorothy Bundy and Don
      McNeill, 6-2, 6-3
1945 Miss Osborne and Talbert d. Doris Hart and Bob Falkenburg,
      6-4, 6-4
1946 Miss Osborne and Talbert d. Miss Brough and Robert Kim-
      brell, 6-3, 6-4

1947   MISS BROUGH and JOHN BROMWICH d. Gussie Moran and Pancho Segura, 6-3, 6-1
1948   MISS BROUGH and TOM BROWN d. Mrs. Margaret Osborne duPont and Talbert, 6-4, 6-4
1949   MISS BROUGH and ERIC STURGESS d. Mrs. duPont and Talbert, 4-6, 6-3, 7-5
1950   MRS. MARGARET OSBORNE DUPONT and KEN MCGREGOR d. Doris Hart and Frank Sedgman, 6-4, 3-6, 6-3
1951   DORIS HART and FRANK SEDGMAN d. Shirley Fry and Mervyn Rose, 6-3, 6-2
1952   MISS HART and SEDGMAN d. Mrs. Thelma Long and Lew Hoad, 6-3, 7-5
1953   MISS HART and VIC SEIXAS d. Julia Ann Sampson and Rex Hartwig, 6-2, 4-6, 6-4
1954   MISS HART and SEIXAS d. Mrs. duPont and Ken Rosewall, 4-6, 6-1, 6-1
1955   MISS HART and SEIXAS d. Shirley Fry and Gardnar Mulloy, 7-5, 5-7, 6-2
1956   MRS. DUPONT and KEN ROSEWALL d. Darlene Hard and Lew Hoad, 9-7, 6-1
1957   ALTHEA GIBSON and KURT NIELSEN d. Darlene Hard and Richard Howe, 6-3, 9-7
1958   MRS. DUPONT and NEALE FRASER d. Maria Bueno and Alex Olmedo, 6-4, 3-6, 9-7
1959   MRS. DUPONT and FRASER d. Janet Hopps and Bob Mark, 7-5, 13-15, 6-2
1960   MRS. DUPONT and FRASER d. Maria Bueno and Antonio Palafox, 6-3, 6-2
1961   MARGARET SMITH and BOB MARK d. Miss Hard and Dennis Ralston by default
1962   MISS SMITH and FRED STOLLE d. Leslie Turner and Frank Froehling, 7-5, 6-2
1963   MISS SMITH and KEN FLETCHER d. Judy Tegart and Ed Rubinoff, 3-6, 8-6, 6-2
1964   MISS SMITH and JOHN NEWCOMBE d. Judy Tegart and Ed Rubinoff, 10-8, 4-6, 6-3
1965   MISS SMITH and STOLLE d. Judy Tegart and Frank Froehling, 6-2, 6-2
1966   MRS. DONNA FALES and OWEN DAVIDSON d. Mrs. Carol Aucamp and Ed Rubinoff, 6-1, 6-3
1967   MRS. BILLIE JEAN KING and DAVIDSON d. Rosemary Casals and Stan Smith, 6-3, 6-2
1968   MARY ANN EISEL and PETER CURTIS d. Tory Fretz and Gerry Perry, 6-4, 7-5

Index

Addie, Pauline Betz, 173
Alcindor, Lew, 27
Allison, Wilmer, 9, 44, 46, 47, 48, 55, 60, 62, 63, 87, 88, 152, 153, 154-55, 156-57, 158, 160, 161
Ashe, Arthur, 69-70, 110, 111, 124, 171, 173
Astaire, Fred, 26
Austin, Bunny, 52-55, 77, 88-89, 109, 115-16, 117, 120, 169

backhand, 110-15
Barnes, Bruce, 132
Beasley, Mercer, 34
Benny, Jack, 6, 14, 18, 19-20
Benson, Mrs. Martin (Jean, sister), 25
Borotra, Jean, 98-99
Bousses, Christian, 52
Bromwich, John, 106, 117-18, 160, 161, 164
Bryan, Lefty, 158
Buchholz, Butch, 124
Budge, Donald (uncle), 22, 23
Budge, John (Jack) (father), 21-24, 31-32
Budge, Lloyd (brother), 24, 26, 30-32, 33
Budge, Lori (wife), 168
Budge, Pearl Kincaid (mother), 21, 24, 174
Burchard, Jim, 130

Carlin, Phil, 32, 85
Casals, Pablo, 107, 108-109
Chamberlain, Wilt, 27

Chapin, Al, 132
Cochet, Henri, 111, 137, 149
Connolly, Maureen, 173
Cramm, Gottfried von, 3, 4, 5, 6, 7, 8-20, 36, 47-48, 52, 53, 55, 56, 63, 72, 73, 76, 77-80, 88-90, 105, 107-108, 149, 157, 158, 160, 169
Crawford, Jack, 60-63, 101, 103, 159, 160

Danzig, Allison, 130, 140
Davis, Dwight F., 44
Dewey, Tom, 141
DiMaggio, Joe, 25, 91-92, 108, 131
Doeg, John, 35, 73-74, 163
Doherty brothers, 168
Dorsey, Tommy, 82
doubles strategy, 154-67
Drobny, Jaroslav, 111, 117, 138, 171
Durr, Françoise, 43

Fabyan, Sarah Palfrey, Mrs., 166
Faunce, John, 170
Feller, Bob, 91, 141
Fitzgibbon, J. J., 170
forehand, 56-59
Froehling, Frank, 124

Gonzales, Pancho, 39, 69, 70, 73, 74, 92-95, 138, 146, 149, 161
Goodman, Benny, 109
Graebner, Clark, 124, 172, 173
Grange, Red, 149
Grant, Bitsy, 4, 6, 7, 14, 42, 44, 45, 46, 60, 77, 114-15, 164
grips, 58-59
Gustav, King of Sweden, 5

Hare, Charles, 76-77, 169
Hare, Mary Hardwicke, 169
Harris, Jack, 126-28, 130-31, 132, 134, 141, 142
Haughton, B. A., 170
Henkel, Henner, 4, 6-7, 14, 46-47, 48, 73, 76, 158, 160
Hitler, Adolf, 3, 5, 7, 8, 19
Hoad, Lew, 102, 103, 171
Hopman, Harry, 166
Hunt, Charles, 36
Hunt, Joe, 36
Hutton, Barbara, 9

Icely, L. B., 127

Jacobs, Helen, 33
Johansson, Torsten, 172
Johnston, Little Billy, 33, 43, 122, 129
Jones, Bobby, 102, 148-49
Jones, Perry, 35

King, Billie Jean, 169, 173
Kingman, Russell, 107, 108
Kinsey, Howard, 163
Kinsey, Robert, 163
Kipling, Rudyard, 174
Kirby, Vernon, 42
Kleinscroth, Heinrich, 169
Kovacs, Frank, 111, 143, 151
Kramer, Jack, 29, 39, 70, 73, 95, 123, 125, 128, 138, 146, 149, 156, 168, 169-70, 171
Kukulevich, Franjo, 107

Laney, Al, 130
Laver, Rod, 29, 39, 73, 80, 102, 103, 110, 149, 162, 169, 171, 173, 174
Lebair, Harold, 118
Lee, Sammy, 170
Lenglen, Suzanne, 122
lob, 164-65
Lott, George, 35, 163
Louis, Joe, 75
Lukas, Paul, 6, 14, 18
Lund, Kay, 9, 47-48
Lutz, Bob, 145

McDiarmid, John, 64, 158
McGregor, Ken, 161

McNeill, Don, 110, 111
Mako, Gene, 7, 36, 44-46, 51, 62, 63, 64, 76, 77, 81-82, 102, 104, 105, 106, 116, 118, 119-21, 151-153, 155, 156-61, 166
Marble, Alice, 25, 33, 69, 77, 108, 116, 166, 173
Martini, Al, 171
Marx, Groucho, 8, 95-96
Match, Sammy, 171
Mays, Willie, 29
Menzel, Roderich, 107, 108
Moody, Helen Wills, 33, 174
Mulloy, Gardnar, 151, 161, 171, 172

Neale, Emory, 170
Near, J. LeRoy, Dr., 144
Nelson, Byron, 102

Okker, Tom, 69
Olmedo, Alex, 145
Osuna, Rafael, 145
overhead, 135-39
Owens, Jesse, 5

Parker, Frankie, 34-35, 36, 42, 60, 64, 77, 95-96, 111, 118, 144, 151, 161, 172
Pasarell, Charlie, 124, 150
Pate, Walter, 4, 12, 14, 44, 45, 61-62, 64, 77, 86-87, 119, 130
Perry, Fred, 5, 9, 12, 13, 42, 48, 55-57, 59, 60, 61, 63-66, 67, 74-75, 76-77, 78, 91, 95-97, 103, 105, 111, 112, 122, 123, 125, 126, 131-132, 140, 142, 143, 149, 169
poaching, 165-66
Pyle, C. C. (Cash and Carry), 122

Queen Mary, 3, 4, 7, 53-54, 116
Quist, Adrian, 52, 62-63, 118, 159, 160

racket selection, 162
Ralston, Dennis, 110, 124, 145, 171
Reed, Whitney, 28-29
Reyes, Esteban, 45-46
Richards, Vinnie, 122, 156
Richey, Cliff, 124
Riessen, Marty, 27, 124
Riggs, Bobby, 39, 84-85, 110-11, 116, 125, 128, 143, 144-46, 149, 151, 164, 166, 169, 172

Roche, Tony, 171, 173
Rosewall, Ken, 103, 110, 149, 162,
    171
Ruth, Babe, 102, 149

Sabin, Wayne, 144
Santana, Manuel, 39, 110, 150
Schroeder, Ted, 138
Sedgman, Frank, 92, 116, 146, 149,
    161-62
Segura, Pancho, 92, 99-100, 149,
    161, 172
serve, 69-74
Shields, Frank, 162-63
Shor, Toots, 91
Smith, Gene, 64
Smith, Stan, 145
Snead, Sammy, 70, 127
Stoefen, Lester, 73, 74, 140
Stow, Tom, 42-43, 60, 75, 76, 77,
    111
Sullivan, Ed, 6, 14, 18

Talbert, Billy, 86, 161

Thompson, Lex, 143
Tilden, Bill, 4, 6, 13-14, 18, 28, 36,
    56, 73, 90, 91, 96, 98-99; 111,
    122, 126, 127, 129, 136, 137, 138,
    140, 142, 148, 149, 151, 156, 170
Tinling, Teddy, 7-8
Toley, George, 145-46
Trabert, Tony, 27, 111

Unitas, Johnny, 29

Van Ryn, John, 9, 44, 47, 88, 153,
    154, 155, 156-57, 158, 160, 161
Vines, Ellsworth, 27, 29, 35, 56, 63,
    64, 69, 70, 73, 74-75, 77, 83, 90-
    91, 104, 122, 125, 126, 127, 131,
    132-33, 134-35, 138-40, 142, 149
volley, 153-54, 166-67

Weir, Joseph, 87-88
Williams, Norris, 156
Williams, Ted, 26
Wingfield, Walter C., 39
Wood, Sidney, 44, 46, 87, 88